SUFFERING

ISSUES OF EMOTIONAL LIVING
IN AN AGE OF STRESS
FOR CLERGY AND RELIGIOUS

THE NINTH
PSYCHOTHEOLOGICAL SYMPOSIUM

JOHN A. STRUZZO

BERNARD J. BUSH

THOMAS A. KANE

RICHARD J. GILMARTIN

RITA D'ANDREA

ANNA POLCINO

J. WILLIAM HUBER

AUDREY E. CAMPBELL-WRAY

EDITED BY RICHARD J. GILMARTIN

AFFIRMATION BOOKS
WHITINSVILLE, MASSACHUSETTS

Affirmation Books is an important part of the ministry of the House of Affirmation, International Therapeutic Center for Clergy and Religious, founded by Sr. Anna Polcino, S.C.M.M., M.D. Income from the sale of Affirmation books and tapes is used to provide care for priests and religious suffering from emotional unrest.

The House of Affirmation provides a threefold program of service, education, and research. Among its services are five residential therapeutic communities and two counseling centers in the United States and one residential center in England. All centers provide nonresidential counseling. The House sponsors a Leadership conference each year during the first week of February and a month-long Institute of Applied Psychotheology during July. More than forty clinical staff members conduct workshops and symposiums throughout the year.

For further information, write or call the administrative offices in Boston, Massachusetts:

The House of Affirmation
22 The Fenway
Boston, Massachusetts 02215
617/266-8792

To
present and former residents
of the House of Affirmation
with love and gratitude.

Published with Ecclesiastical Permission

First Edition
©1984 by House of Affirmation, Inc.

Library of Congress Cataloging in Publication Data
Psychotheological Symposium, 9th, 1983, Fontbonne Academy, etc.
   Suffering: issues of emotional living in an age of stress for clergy and religious.
   1. Suffering — Religious aspects — Christianity — Congresses.
I. Struzzo, John A.   II. Gilmartin, Richard J.   III.   Title.
BT732.7.P78   1983   233   84-9334

ISBN 0-89571-020-X

Printed by
Mercantile Printing Company, Worcester, Massachusetts
United States of America

CONTENTS

Foreword

Just as this book was about to be sent to the printer, our Holy Father issued a wonderful teaching on suffering. His 13,000 word apostolic letter, dated February 11, 1984, the feast of Our Lady of Lourdes, addresses the entire Church as he affirms that human suffering brings people closer to God by opening them to grace, and in that way completes the work of Christ's redemptive acts. Its Latin title is "Salvifici Doloris," "On the Christian Meaning of Suffering."

The Pope states that suffering, while undoubtedly linked to evil, has a saving power that is understood in Christ's passion. He also stresses ministering to the suffering. Efforts to relieve human suffering are an essential aspect of culture, but individual human compassion has no equal in dealing with the suffering of another. The letter touches on a frequent theme of Pope John Paul's pontificate: while suffering is always a trial, it also calls people to perseverance and reveals human dignity.

The letter also shows papal concern over the threat of nuclear war. That threat, he states, is linked to the "collective meaning" of suffering. The last two world wars brought a "harvest of death" and immense human suffering. He writes:

> The second half of our century, in its turn, brings with it
> — as though in proportion to the mistakes and transgres-
> sions of our contemporary civilization — such a horrible
> threat of nuclear war that we cannot think of this period
> except in terms of an incomparable accumulation of suffer-
> ings, even to the possible self-destruction of humanity.

Not all suffering, the Pope writes, can be understood as the consequence of punishment for the faults of individuals or society. But he adds that suffering cannot be divorced from the sinful background of human history. At the basis of human suffering, he states, "there is a complex involvement with sin."

The passion of Christ, he reminds us, is the key to an individual's understanding of why he or she suffers. Christ's death on the cross brought an end to "definitive suffering," or the loss of eternal life. With Christ's sacrifice, suffering "entered into a completely new dimension and a new order: it has been linked to love." By sharing in the sufferings of Christ, people share in the redemption and become mature enough to enter the kingdom of God, giving suffering a "creative character." The Pope states:

> Suffering has a special value in the eyes of the Church. It is something good, before which the Church bows down in reverence with all the depth of her faith in the redemption.

A special grace that draws people closer to God is often found in suffering.

> It is suffering, more than anything else, which clears the way for the grace which transforms human souls. Suffering, more than anything else, makes present in the history of humanity the powers of the redemption.

Individuals often see their suffering as useless, the Pope states.

> This feeling not only consumes the person interiorly, but seems to make him a burden to others. The person feels condemned to receive help and assistance from others, and at the same time seems useless to himself.
> The discovery of the salvific meaning of suffering in union with Christ transforms this depressing feeling.

Helping to relieve suffering, on the other hand, is the perfect way for a person to "find himself by making a sincere gift of himself," Pope John Paul writes. He goes on: "Christ has taught us to do good by his suffering and to do good to those who suffer. In this double aspect he has completely revealed the meaning of suffering." The task of relieving suffering does not stop at sympathy, the Pope states, but must be carried to effective social action involving families, schools and individuals.

The House of Affirmation is a ministry born out of the suffering and healing of many priests and religious. Affirmation Books is an important part of this ministry. Dr. Richard Gilmartin was one of the first persons to join Sister Anna Polcino, M.D., and myself when we first began this ministry in 1970. It is appropriate that Dr. Gilmartin, who ministers to many suffering priests and religious, is the editor of this volume. I hope the reflections that this man of faith and science has brought together will serve to challenge the thought and encourage the faith of the readers of Affirmation books.

Thomas A. Kane, Ph.D., D.P.S.

Priest, Diocese of Worcester
Publisher, Affirmation Books
Whitinsville, Massachusetts

19 March 1984
Feast of St. Joseph

Preface

Suffering is as much a part of the human experience as is birth, growth, and death. No one of us is exempt. It may be suffering of the body as is experienced in disease and illness, accident or aging; suffering of the mind as in depression, anxiety, loss, or the burden of an unwanted part of the self; or suffering of the spirit as in sin, alienation, and a loss of the sense of the divine in our lives. Suffering moves in and out of our lives. For some of us, suffering is the discordant notes in the symphony of life, for others the contra-point which accents the melody, and for still others the theme which gives substance to the entire work. Although we may commit our lives to alleviating the suffering of others, none of us escapes it.

The ninth annual House of Affirmation symposium examines the topic of suffering. The present volume *Suffering: Issues of Emotional Living in an Age of Stress for Clergy and Religious*, invites all of us to examine with the staff of the House of Affirmation the many facets of suffering in the life of a Christian. Suffering can be the cause of personal destruction or an invitation to personal growth. The value or meaning of suffering is contingent upon our personal response when suffering enters our lives. It is never a friend, but it need not be an enemy. It can be a source of meaning in our lives; it can gift us with compassion for our fellow sufferers; and it can call us to work for the eradication of suffering in the lives of our oppressed brothers and sisters. We see how suffering can be expressed through our creativity, and how it can unite us to the Suffering Christ.

Gratitude goes to those speakers who presented papers at the Boston, San Francisco, Saint Louis, and Clearwater symposiums. I also wish to thank the men and women who attended the sessions. Their presence, attention, receptivity, and response provided the atmosphere within which the ideas presented were developed. As there would be no great poetry without people who love great poetry, so too there would be no original thinking without people who love original ideas.

Many contributed to the success of these symposiums, especially the behind-the-scenes people who make our symposium days smooth and pleasant experiences. There are too many workers to mention individually, but to all my sincere thanks. A special mention must be made, however, of the symposium moderators who, besides introducing the speakers and moderating the discussions, set the tone for each of the days: Father John Allan Loftus, S.J., Ph.D. (Boston); Dr. Audrey Campbell-Wray (San Francisco); Sister Kathleen Kelley, S.N.D.de N. (Saint Louis); and Father Gerald Fath, O.P., D.Min. (Clearwater).

We are also grateful to those who extended hospitality for the meetings: the Sisters of Saint Joseph at Fontbonne Academy in Milton, Massachusetts; the Sisters of the Presentation in San Francisco; the staff of Saint John's Mercy Hospital in Saint Louis; and the clergy and religious of the Diocese of St. Petersburg, Florida.

Finally, as in other years, we dedicate this new volume in the symposium series to our past and present residents. We are thankful for their gifts, promising a future of continued growth and love.

Richard J. Gilmartin, Ph.D.

House of Affirmation
Whitinsville, Massachusetts

16 February 1984

Suffering: Its Pain and Its Gift

John A. Struzzo

- Mind – Body Connection • Roots of Suffering
- Physical Suffering • Suffering as Career
- The Role of Family in Suffering
- Suffering and Emotions
- Suffering: Opportunity for Growth
- Suffering: Its Alleviation and Healing
- Energy • Blocked Energy • Energization

Reverend John A. Struzzo, C.S.C., Ph.D., is a full-time psychotherapist at the House of Affirmation in Montara, California. A priest of the Congregation of Holy Cross, Fr. Struzzo received his bachelor's and master's degrees in theology and sociology at the University of Notre Dame and his doctorate in sociology from Florida State University. For several years Fr. Struzzo was Professor of Sociology at Northern Illinois University. He then completed a postgraduate certificate in marriage and family psychotherapy at the Institute of Religion and Health in New York City, and interned in clinical psychology at Worcester State Hospital. Before joining the staff of the House of Affirmation, Fr. Struzzo was executive director of a pastoral counseling center in South Bend, Indiana. He has lectured widely on issues relating to psychology and religion, and on personal growth and development. He is a member of the American Association of Pastoral Counselors, the American Association of Marriage and Family Therapists, and the California Association of Marriage and Family Therapy.

Introduction

The language we use to talk about suffering suggests both its meaning and the process of its alleviation. We make statements like: We suffer from a cold; we suffer hangovers; we suffer grief and depression; we suffer the heat or cold. Each of these uses of the word "suffering" assumes a passive stance and expresses our point of view as victims who have something impinging on us from the outside. Consequently, our emotional state is one of helplessness rather than response.

One of the basic roots of suffering is the belief that we are helpless. Such belief shuts down personal energy. To illustrate this, say to yourself "I can't." Say it over and over until you are aware of the underlying feeling of those words. Now say, "I choose not to." Finally say, "Each day I'm becoming more and more competent." What is the difference between the three statements? In the first instance, "I can't" tends to create a feeling of helplessness and a sense of low energy, energy which is also constricted. When we take responsibility for our behavior by saying, "I choose not to," we feel a greater flow of energy and some sense of power. In the last example, we feel our energy opening outward with a sense of hope.

Suffering is rooted both in low energy and in feelings of helplessness.

Health is based on both high energy and feelings of power and hope.

Mind – Body Connection

Recently during a restful morning I was enjoying being deeply engrossed in a book. I eventually looked at my watch. It was two o'clock. I realized I had not eaten lunch. All of a sudden, I felt hungry. Until that moment, I had not felt hungry. In fact, a short time earlier I had been consciously aware that I was not hungry. However, in my mind I equate noon with lunch. Therefore, I *thought hungry* at two. Aware of my hunger pangs because it was two o'clock, I said to myself, "I don't have to be hungry,'' and decided not to eat right then. My hunger dissipated. This experience once again made me aware of how human suffering originates in the mind.

Our thoughts can create our feelings. Mental events are accompanied by corresponding physical events, and every physical event has an effect on one's mind. To further illustrate this, say quietly to yourself, ''I need you to love me.'' Now, once you are aware of your feelings, change the statement to, ''I feel your love for me.'' What is the difference? In the first instance, we tend to feel emptiness and deprivation. In the second case, we tend to feel warmth and joy. This connection between body and mind has been graphically shown by Dr. Michael Lieberman in his study of unborn children. Dr. Lieberman found that a fetus became emotionally agitated (measured by increased heartbeat) each time an expectant mother even thought of having a cigarette.[1]

At the same time, our very body posture both reflects and influences our mental state. For example, someone who is passive and shrinks from the world will likely assume a posture expressing that attitude. Likewise if a person assumes a critical posture, and that stance becomes habitual, it can actually sustain and perpetuate the underlying emotional and mental state. Thus people who tighten and raise their shoulders when they feel defensive may begin to habitually develop, and later maintain, this stance. Eventually even in situations when people ordinarily relax, these individuals continue to control and restrict their shoulder muscles. Such constant tension will increasingly create feelings of fear and defensiveness. Muscles serve as memory banks for various emotional and mental states. This is the premise behind most body therapies. Both posture and muscle constriction not only reflect character, but actually sustain it; and in doing so may either assist or hinder growth and development.[2]

Consequently, suffering is much more the result of our attitudes and beliefs than of external circumstances. Likewise if

one part of the body suffers, the whole person suffers. Ultimately individual suffering can be understood only in reference
to total personal reality — physical, psychological, social and
spiritual.

Roots of Suffering

In essence, suffering is the result of both our attachments and
ignorance. We suffer because we base our expectation of happiness on the fulfillment of desires.

You have been in a situation where you are walking down a
street on a beautiful warm, sunny day. You are enjoying the air
and feeling very content. Then you pass a store window, and
see an object you want. You begin to wish you had that object
and start suffering deprivation feelings. The assumption is, if
only I could have that object, I would be happy. If only I had a
new car, a better job, an ideal friend, better food, good sex; if
only I were more beautiful or handsome, weighed less, or whatever, the list goes on and on, I would be happy. Because of our
desires, we feel deprived and therefore, experience suffering.
We usually think of happiness as the result of some external
fulfillment — material possessions or goals realized.

This ignorance of our true nature results in suffering. We
tend to think of ourselves as bodies that have souls. The reality
is, we are souls — spiritual beings — that have bodies which
manifest our spiritual reality. Our physical bodies are transitory
and will end at death. In this sense, our bodies are illusions. If
we assume that our bodies are our true natures then we believe
the fulfillment of external needs and desires will bring us true
happiness. Our true fulfillment lies beyond Earth. Desires and
attachments anchor us to Earth. Suffering then is a result of our
ignorance — of our too restricted consciousness.[3] Consider that
if joy were constant on Earth and there were no suffering, the
hope of a much fuller and happier life beyond Earth would be
forgotten.[4]

At the same time however, we must not forget or ignore the
human side of our mind – body connection. Before we can free
ourselves from desires and attachments, we first need to be

grounded in body, in ego, in our earthbound selves in order to become comfortable with ourselves, our bodies. Spiritual masters warn of the great dangers that can result from an extreme focus on spiritual development without corresponding physical, emotional and psychological development.[5]

Religious who take the vow of celibacy without first being grounded in an awareness and acceptance of sexuality create an imbalance between the spiritual, emotional and physical aspects of their total personality. Celibacy is a transformation of sexual energy into a creative bond with God and with all creation. To control and then to renounce this energy and to transform it without first coming to know it, opens the way for physical and mental disorders.[6] Repressed sexual energy can result in frustration or negative attitudes and beliefs. As John Sanford writes, the process of individuation can take place only if "our conscious personality develops and increases, and becomes a channel for the life of the whole person to flow through." If life energies are blocked and thwarted, they turn against us. In this lies the potential for illness, and therefore, suffering.[7]

Physical Suffering

The most common experience of suffering is physical pain. However, pain itself is not suffering in the sense used here. Such pain is rather a personal, subjective experience. While such pain is real and experienced as suffering by most people, I want to probe deeper into the meaning of suffering. In order to do that, I am going to focus on physical pain experienced as suffering.

Over a century ago, Sir William Osler instructed his students: "Ask not what kind of illness the patient has, but what kind of patient has the illness?"[8] Physical pain may be a metaphor of our psychological, emotional and spiritual reality. People often express their emotional and spiritual conflicts through physical illness.[9]

When we were children growing up, we learned that suffering can have many rewards. We learned, for example, that a headache may mean missing school and avoiding a test. A stomachache may mean getting special attention from mother. How others respond to our pain can determine whether an acute though transient pain will become a chronic liability. What happens when you say, "I hurt"? Do others listen attentively and show sympathy? Do they excuse you from participating further in your regular responsibilities at work, or in the family? Do they cease being angry at you, and give you a lot of attention? Or do they refuse to listen to you, or accuse you of faking it? Do they judge that you are simply shirking responsibilities?[10]

If suffering yields sought after consequences, then it is reinforced, and the chances of the suffering recurring are increased. Thus people can learn to be ill and express pain, and therefore suffer. For example, a husband may realize that his wife becomes more attentive and tender when he expresses pain, and when he feels good, she ignores him. In this way, the wife is teaching the husband to suffer pain.[11]

Suffering can be learned to serve many functions. It can get us out of doing something we do not want to do. Suffering can get us special attention and nurturance. It can be a defense. For example a mother says to her child, "Not now, honey. I have a headache." The headache may be a defense against the demands of childcare and a way to avoid saying, "No, I don't want to give you attention right now."

Suffering as Career

Once we learn suffering may have desirable consequences, either assumed or real, we can make a career of suffering. Dr. Szasz describes such men and women as seeking advanced degrees in pain.[12] Once people unconsciously adopt a career in suffering, they develop skills in manipulating others both in their family and in the health profession in order to validate their pain. The most minimal validation is a periodic visit to the doctor. However, the best way to validate a career in pain is periodic operations. For example, a patient who complains of a chronic stomachache may have an appendectomy.

People who are sophisticated in their suffering career will seek the collaboration of specialists, usually orthopedists or general surgeons. At the height of their careers, sufferers will seek out neurosurgeons.[13]

Collaboration between a sufferer and a physician is necessary for the maintenance and periodic validation of a career of suffering. In the medical profession, the presumption is in favor of illness, and if a doctor conducts enough tests, some abnormality will be found. The fear of malpractice suits further motivates the physician to make sure nothing is missed. A doctor recently told me that about two thirds of his cases are more psychologically than physically afflicted. Boredom and depression are two common underlying issues. However, because most patients do not want to hear this, their physical symptoms are treated. Prescriptions for drugs also confirm an assumed illness. Consequently, physicians may inadvertently reinforce a patient's illness and collude in a self-fulfilling prophecy.[14]

Not only do doctors collaborate but also lawyers and insurance claimants contribute to increase the amount and length of suffering and may even create it in the first place. As Dr. Pace points out, pain that is a result of industrial accidents is especially difficult to treat because of the potentiality for litigation, compensation and various types of financial rewards.[15] In industrial accidents the patient often feels, "I'll show those guys how bad I feel and how much I suffer," and at the same time, "I'll make them pay for it." Such thinking hinders any attempt at treatment.[16]

To illustrate, Dr. Pace reports that in cases of back injuries suffered in industrial accidents, if a suitable course of therapy is initiated within six weeks, then eighty percent of the injured will return to full employment. If litigation or referrals to other consultants postpones treatment for six months, then only fifty percent recover. If the process drags on for more than one year, then only about five percent will return to full employment.[17]

The Role of Family in Suffering

The family structure plays a large role in both suffering and subsequent health. Dr. Salvador Minunchin has concluded from his research and experience that the ill family member is often a scapegoat for conflicts within the home. The other family members can feel better because they can focus their energy on the child and thereby avoid facing their own conflicts. To protect the family, the child has to remain sick.[18] From my experience as a family counselor, it seems that when a family is in trouble the most sensitive child may be the bearer of the pain. This seems especially true when the parents are having difficulty with their relationship. By identifying one of the children as the patient, they can avoid facing their own marital relationship.

Several years ago, I was counseling both parents and their three children, two boys and a girl. The identified patient was the middle child, whom we will call Mark. Mark was 14 and had a sister 19 and a younger brother 12. Mark was constantly getting into trouble both at school and at home. His grades were poor and he frequently skipped classes. When he did attend, he was consistently disruptive. At home he would steal, smoke pot and in general refused to cooperate with any of his parents' wishes. He finally was caught by the police for vandalizing a neighbor's property. His parents brought him to me for counseling. I asked to see the whole family. Through my interviews with the family, it became clear that the problem was in the total family system, and that Mark was acting out that problem. Mark was very handsome, charming and sensual in a family that was basically dead. He was the most feeling member. It also became clear that the mother had a strong emotional bond with Mark that had a lot of sexual undertones. For example, she visited him frequently in his room at night before he went to sleep. He would be lying in bed in his underwear, and she would be wearing a bathrobe. She also regularly woke him in the morning. Frequently, he would oversleep, miss his school bus, and mother would drive him to school. When I suggested getting Mark his own alarm clock, the mother gave all kinds of excuses why that would not work. It further became evident through our sessions that her husband was not satisfying her either emotionally or sexually. Also the father was very distant from Mark. Unconsciously, Mark became the husband for the mother, and the object of the mother's emotional and sexual needs. Mark desperately wanted a male role model. I finally encouraged the mother to become less involved in Mark's life while having his father become more involved. Mark began to change, and his mother began to complain to her husband about his lack of emotional involvement with her. Eventually they were able to face that the real problem was their relationship and Mark was bearing the pain of that relationship. Also Mark by his behavior was trying to pull the family toward health. He was the only one really alive in that family.

Dr. Minunchin has observed that psychosomatically ill children tend to be in strongly enmeshed families where there are few personal boundaries. Thus, members frequently invade one another's private lives. Once a child becomes sick, the whole family tends to become overprotective.[19] Their response tends to reinforce the illness. Families like any social system try to maintain their status quo, and avoid change. Thus, if one member of a family changes, and the family system has not changed, it is likely that another member will begin to express the symptoms of the family's distress. The difficulties of individual members manifest a family's conflicts.

Suffering and Emotions

One of the main contributing factors to physical illness is repressed emotions. Thomas Holmes investigated the emotional life-situations of several patients with colds. He found that frequently repressed feelings, such as anger, preceded the onset of minor illness. He also discovered that during the discussion of emotionally difficult circumstances, nasal congestion increased.[20] My own clinical experience is that sinus congestion is often linked to unresolved grief feelings.

Ellerbrock observed that when he was talking to acne patients, they would consistently scratch themselves when under emotional stress. He eventually associated the itching with the feeling of "being picked on." He concluded that acne may be a reaction to "being picked on, nagged at, and wanting to be left alone."[21] He further noticed that if the victimized feeling was expressed in depression, the itching did not occur.

Psychosomatic illness experts, W.J. Grace and D.T. Graham, conducted in-depth interviews with 128 patients to probe the connection between their life situations and their physical symptoms. He found that patients with diarrhea tended to want to get rid of something, or end a situation. For example, one man developed diarrhea after buying a car that was a lemon. Patients with constipation were grimly determined to persevere, even though they faced insurmountable obstacles. For example, one person said, "My marriage is never going to work, but I won't quit." Constipation is a bodily process of holding on to substances without change, despite bodily discomfort.[22] Not only may the body clog up, but also the emotions. There is emotional and mental constipation too. Basically constipation is a way of holding in our energy. Thus certain mental attitudes are constipating like "I can't do it" or "I am no good." Again contrast the feeling of energy when you say, "I can't" as opposed to "I can do it." One restricts energy; the other expands it.

Another attitude that can be constipating is perfectionism. The belief that I have to do it perfectly often prevents any motion at all, and is paralyzing. Constipating attitudes lead to feelings of helplessness, and sometimes hopelessness. As a result, on the spiritual level, a person may tend to see life as meaningless, and question God's love and presence. Our mental and spiritual states manifest in our physical state. Many chronic diseases can begin when a person feels unable to cope with certain emotional stresses and strains, or to deal effectively with something disliked. Alleviation of suffering, therefore, requires change at all levels of personality — body, mind and spirit.[23]

For example, research shows that chronic sufferers are people who tend to neglect their deepest human needs — the need for touching, the need for companionship, the need for sharing inner feelings, the need for sexual fulfillment, the need for personal validation through the giving and receiving of love. In general, sufferers' lives are characterized by duty and obligation to others, usually people who give little in return.[24] The healthier persons are, the more they are aware of their emotional and psychological needs. Likewise, the less healthy are less able to directly express needs.[25]

In my opinion, negative feelings, especially fear, anger and guilt, underpinned by a lack of self-love, are the greatest causes of physical suffering. These negative feelings are mirrored in our bodies.[26]

A few years ago I was supervising a priest on pastoral care. He went to visit a woman who was undergoing a masectomy. Before the surgery, she was all smiles trying to cheer up the staff and the rest of the patients. After the surgery, she remained all smiles, joking with the nurses. At the same time, she was not healing. The head nurse told the priest that this patient was driving everyone crazy. The priest provoked the patient into getting angry. Not only did she get angry at him, but she began to curse the doctors, nurses and even God. She also began to heal. Her denied anger and underlying fear had blocked her energy and in turn her healing potential.

Suffering: Opportunity for Growth

Although suffering is never beneficial in itself, and thus cannot be a direct goal of our life, suffering does provide an opportunity for growth. What is important is how we react in the face of suffering.[27] In his discussion of "creative suffering," Dr. Paul Tournier recalls one holiday he had to spend alone in a hotel room. He felt bitter about being there and passively suffered the loneliness. Finally, he shifted his whole attitude and welcomed the opportunity, and his suffering was transformed into a sweet solitude.[28]

It is not enough to resign oneself to the inevitable. To truly accept suffering means expressing an active and positive Yes! to life. It means getting inside the suffering and committing oneself totally to the present moment.[29] To seek suffering is morbid and destructive; but to run away from it is cowardly.

Every experience of suffering carries within it a lesson. Each of us has an inner guide, a guide that knows what we need to be healthy, whole, integrated, loving persons. We must learn to respond to the guide within us. As we do this, we will learn certain basic lessons. Our life situations help us learn those lessons. Suffering is a teaching life situation. We can see suffering as a hindrance and thus become frustrated, fearful and angry. Or we can look at suffering as an opportunity to correct past mistakes, and learn the lessons it offers us. Instead of asking, why me? or why am I suffering?, help yourself by asking: what is the lesson this particular experience of suffering is trying to teach me? or what can I learn about myself from it?

Once we perceive suffering as opportunity, we increase our energy and direct our attitudes and feelings more positively. Once we open ourselves to the lessons that suffering can teach us, our need to suffer diminishes.[30]

Suffering is not creative in itself. However, we are seldom creative without suffering. Suffering is an opportunity for creativity.[31] Often when I experience people as full of compassion and sensitivity, I discover they have learned those qualities through creatively struggling with intense suffering.

In the discussion so far, I have put great emphasis on the mind – body connection, the role of the mind and spirit in physical suffering. Yogananda, one of the great spiritual teachers of our century, has said that physical suffering does not always bring mental agony if the mind is strong, but mental suffering ususally brings physical suffering. When the soul is sick, both mind and body suffer.[32] John Mumford writes, ''Our mental state is reflected in the function, control and appearance of our physical being.''[33] Suffering occurs in a complex milieu of psychological, psychosocial and interpersonal relationships.[34] Suffering is basically the result of an imbalance between our physical, mental, emotional, and spiritual parts. The alleviation of suffering and the process of total health require the restoration of that balance.

Suffering: Its Alleviation and Healing

Energy

Both suffering and healing are a matter of energy. Einstein has helped us to realize that all matter is energy and that all energy is matter. Furthermore, the smallest particle of matter contains a tremendous amount of concentrated energy as evidenced by nuclear fusion.[35] The more mindful we are that all matter is a manifestation of energy, the more we will be able to control and transcend matter, and thereby conquer fatigue, disease and suffering. Energy is the link between body, mind and spirit.

When we experience suffering, our energy is low. We experience suffering as moving downward, as a heavy feeling. Even our eyes tend to look downward. Our posture reflects this attitude. On the other hand when we feel good, we experience our energy rising, and we tend to look upward. Thus the more energy we have and the more we channel its flow by focusing it with awareness and concentration, the more we will be able to heal ourselves and alleviate suffering. When our energy is low or blocked, we become susceptible to disease. For when we constrict, block or deplete our energy, we also shut down our immune system and become vulnerable to illness.

Blocked Energy

Normally our energy flows smoothly. This flow is experienced as emotion. When we repress or attempt to directly control our emotions or our sexual instinct, our muscles contract, and our free flow of energy is inhibited. Wilhelm Reich developed the concept of armoring to describe the muscular constriction we use against the breakthrough of emotions and instincts, especially fear, rage and sexual excitation.[36] Negative thoughts and their consequent negative feelings are a major factor in blocking our energy and are as a result conducive to our susceptibility to disease. Similarly, Russian philosopher Gurdjieff argues that a restless body and a restless mind with their underlying fear and anxiety are major sources of energy depletion.[37]

Energization

If energy is fundamental to health and happiness, how do we increase our energy and promote our well-being? First, we need to identify and remove the blocks that impede the flow of energy within us. On the physical level, we need to dissolve our armoring by alleviating chronic muscular contractions which interfere with the free flow of energy. By doing this, we restore our bodies" natural healing power.[38] There are several body therapies that deal directly with muscle tension by using breathing, physical manipulation, movement and relaxation techniques.[39] Such therapy can integrate the body and mind.

Also proper diet, exercise and elimination are important physical aspects of increased energy.[40] In general, we need to love and accept our body and listen to the guide of its natural wisdom. Our body knows what it needs.[41]

On the mental level, we need to become aware of the negative programs, thoughts, and beliefs that constrict and deplete our energy. We know that saying "I can't," and harboring negative emotions such as fear, anger and guilt rob us of energy. To increase our energy, we must change our negative thoughts and programs into positive affirmations about ourselves, and others, and God.

It means a wholehearted Yes! to life. Our attitude toward each day begins with our first waking moment. What are our first thoughts when our alarms ring? Do we say, Oh no, not seven o'clock already? Do we pull the covers over our heads? Or do we greet the day with gratitude and a Yes! to God — I am awake and ready to greet every opportunity this day affords me. Such a positive affirmation opens us to an ever expanding flow of energy, and sets the tone for the rest of our day. Throughout the day, we can convert negative thoughts into positive attitudes. For example, if you feel failure, say to yourself: I have all I need to be a success; each day I am becoming more and more successful. When you want to feel healthy, affirm that you *are* healthy. If we judge these suggestions hypocritical and Pollyannish, we perpetuate our ignorance of our true reality. In reality, we have everything we need to be happy. We are already perfect because we share in God's life and energy. Energy is God's life manifest in us. Thus our source of energy is limitless. It is belief in our spiritual reality that is the main source of energy in our lives.

One of the most significant aids in helping us to realize our spiritual nature is meditation. Meditation techniques enable us to relax and center ourselves. As we relax, we energize, and our concentration improves. Religious meditation is a way of focusing our concentrated energy on one thought — God. If you focus sunlight with a magnifying glass, you can burn a hole in a piece of paper. Likewise our concentrated and focused energy has tremendous power. In meditation, spiritual masters may focus energy at the heart or at the point between the eyebrows, the spiritual eye.

Before we can focus our energy, we need a sufficient flow. By learning to quiet our breathing and to still our bodies and minds, we can transcend our material bodies and realize that we are spiritual beings who are one with God.[42] However, the root causes of suffering, our desires and attachments, distract us and siphon off our energy. Yet, before we can detach ourselves from our desires, we need to attach ourselves to something more exciting and attractive — God. Meditation is a helpful and necessary aid toward detachment and the transformation of suffering into joy. Research on the effect of meditation on the body has documented how in deep states of meditation, people have not been able to feel pain and have even stopped bleeding.[43] Research has also shown the healing power

of meditation on the body, mind and spirit.[44] As William Johnston suggests, human energy is "the material basis for a higher,
unmeasurable, spiritual energy that builds the earth."[45]

Meditation also has its dangers. Since our body, mind, and
spirit are intimately connected, they need to be in tune with one
another. If we therefore focus too much energy in the spiritual
realm without a corresponding growth in the physical and psychological areas, then both physical and mental disorders can
arise. Also as we meditate, our unconscious begins to surface.
Whatever unresolved conflicts exist within us will become conscious, similar to the process of psychotherapy.[46]

St. Augustine wrote that in order to successfully explore the
supernatural world, one must first have a strong foundation in
the natural world. Thomas Merton likewise says, "Meditation
has no point and no reality unless it is firmly rooted in life."[47]
Meditation can also become a means of escapism, where one
flees from responsibilities and from reality itself.[48]

The real worth of meditation is shown by its fruits. The fruits
of the spirit are "love, joy, peace, patience, kindness, goodness, faithfulness, gentleness and self-control."[49] Meditation is
healing when it manifests these fruits in our everyday lives. To
protect us from the potential dangers of meditation, a spiritual
guide or teacher is often helpful, and for most, necessary.

Conclusion
The pain of suffering is real. Suffering can be seen as hardship
or as a gift. It can be looked upon as a hindrance or an opportunity. Suffering endured passively with grim determination
only produces bitterness and cold, distant and defensive relationships with ourselves and others. Suffering accepted actively
with joy leads to compassion and understanding. Suffering is
an invitation to growth, to learning the necessary lessons we
need to realize total health and happiness. The greatest suffering is the fear of suffering — our fear of being vulnerable. By
directly facing our fear and actively accepting our suffering

with love, we discover our true selves. And in that discovery, we find our God and the Christ in each of us. In this mutual discovery, we realize community. Shared pain, which is heard and understood and accepted, leads to intimacy and love. In this shared understanding, we realize our oneness within ourselves, among others, and with our God.

Endnotes

1. Thomas Verny and John Kelly, *The Secret Life of the Unborn Child* (New York: Delta Books, 1981), p. 20.

2. Swami Rama, Rudloph Ballentine and Swami Ajoya, *Yoga and Psychotherapy* (Honesdale, Penn.: Himalayan International Institute, 1979), pp. 3 and 4.

3. Paramahansa Yogananda, *The Science of Religion* (Los Angeles, Calif.: Self-Realization Fellowship, 1982), pp. 21 – 24.

4. Paramahansa Yogananda, *Autobiography of a Yogi* (Los Angeles, Calif.: Self-Realization Fellowship, 1979), p. 320.

5. Motoyama, Hiroshi, *Theories of the Chakras* (Wheaton, Ill.: Theosophical Publishing House, 1981), p. 206.

6. *See* John Struzzo, "Intimate Relationships: Heterosexual and Homosexual," in *Relationships*, ed. Sean Sammon, (Whitinsville, Mass.: Affirmation Books, 1983), pp. 98 and 99 for more discussion. For a more thorough treatise, *see also* Elisabeth Haich, *Sexual Energy and Yoga* (New York: Asi Publishers, Inc., 1975), especially pp. 55 – 61.

7. John Sanford, *Healing and Wholeness* (New York: Paulist Press, 1977), p. 17.

8. Dennis T. Jaffe, *Healing From Within* (New York: Alfred A. Knopf, 1980), p. 27.

9. Ibid., p. 24.

10. J. Blair Pace, M.D., *Pain a Personal Experience* (Chicago: Nelson-Hall, 1976), p. 63.

11. Ibid., p. 64.

12. Ibid., p. 56.

13. Ibid.

14. Jaffe, *Healing From Within*, p. 61.

15. Pace, *Pain a Personal Experience*, pp. 43 and 44.

16. Ibid., p. 45.

17. Ibid., pp. 45 and 46.

18. Salvador Minunchin, *Families and Family Therapy* (Cambridge, Mass.: Harvard University Press, 1976).

19. Ibid., pp. 6 – 8.

20. Jaffe, *Healing From Within*, p. 120.
21. Ibid., p. 115.
22. Ibid., p. 122.
23. Ibid., p. 123.
24. Ibid., p. 125.
25. Ibid., p. 126.
26. Betty Bethards, *Techniques for Health and Wholeness* (Novato, Calif.: Inner Light Foundation, 1979), p. 40.
27. Paul Tournier, *Creative Suffering* (San Francisco: Harper and Row, 1982), p. 37.
28. Ibid., p. 72.
29. Ibid., p. 88 – 90.
30. Bethards, *Techniques for Health and Wholeness*. *See also* Betty Bethards, *Be Your Own Guru* (Novato, Calif.: Inner Light Foundation, 1982).
31. Tournier, *Creative Suffering*, p. 110.
32. Paramahansa Yogananda, *The Second Coming of Christ* (Los Angeles, Calif.: Self-Realization Fellowship, 1979), p. 164.
33. John Mumford, *Psychosomatic Yoga* (New York: Samuel Weiser, 1974), p. 11.
34. Pace, *Pain a Personal Experience*, p. 34.
35. Gary Zukav, *The Dancing Wu Li Masters* (New York: William Morrow, 1979), pp. 176 and 177.
36. Elsworth Baker, *Man in the Trap* (New York: Collier Books, 1980), p. 8.
37. Raymond Van Over, *Total Meditation* (New York: Collier Books, 1978), p. 138.
38. Baker, *Man in the Trap*, p. 45.
39. *See* Gerald Kogan, ed., *Your Body Works* (Berkeley, Calif.: And/Or Press and Transformation Press, 1981), for a good overview of body therapies.
40. *See* Rudolph Ballentine, M.D., *Diet and Nutrition: A Holistic Approach* (Honesdale, Penn.: The Himalayan International Institute, 1978), for a more thorough discussion of nutrition in a holistic perspective.

41. *See* Thomas Hanna, *Bodies in Revolt* (San Francisco, Calif.: Holt, Rinehart and Winston, 1970), for further discussion.

42. *See* Swami Rama, et al., *Science of Breath* (Honesdale, Penn.: The Himalayan International Institute, 1981), for an insightful discussion of breathing. (Controlling one's breath is an important part of quieting one's mind and body. Breath is basically energy.)

43. Van Over, *Total Meditation,* pp. 101 – 120.

44. William Johnston, *Silent Music: The Science of Meditation* (San Francisco, Calif.: Harper and Row, 1979).

45. Ibid., p. 113.

46. Van Over, *Total Meditation,* pp. 153– 62.

47. Ibid., p. 156.

48. Johnston, *Silent Music,* p. 93.

49. Ibid., p. 101.

All Creation Groans

Bernard J. Bush

- Suffering: The Universal Experience
- The *Why?* of Suffering • The *How?* • The *When?*
- The Meaning within Death • The Mystery within Death

Reverend Bernard J. Bush, S.J., Ph.D. (cand.), is director of the House of Affirmation in Montara, California. A member of the California Province of the Society of Jesus who was ordained in 1965, Father Bush studied theology at Regis College, Willowdale, Ontario. He served as student chaplain at the University of San Francisco before assuming the post of spiritual director at the Jesuit theologate in Berkeley, California. From there he went to Boston State Hospital where he interned in pastoral psychology. In 1974 he joined the staff of the House of Affirmation and opened its Boston office. Father Bush has written numerous articles concerning spirituality and social justice, most notably in The Way. *He has been active in the directed retreat movement and has lectured on Ignatian spirituality, religious life, mental health, and social justice.*

Introduction

This is undoubtedly one of the most difficult subjects I have
ever tried to address. I have felt considerable resistance to
explore, reflect on, and share these thoughts on suffering. I am
sure that part of my resistance has to do with the fact that our
ministry in the House of Affirmation deals constantly with people who are suffering. We are always in the presence of suffering, and we suffer too. The term "the wounded healer"
suggests itself. It does apply to this ministry. We are continually
confronted with our own helplessness, our inadequacies, our
personal limitations, and our difficulties from our own inner
conflicts and pains. Even as we are ministering and helping
other people face their own pain and suffering, our own is ever-
present. It is hard work in the sense that it is always an interior
challenge.

I have asked myself what special words do I have about suffering when each of us is expert in suffering in our individual
ways. Any adult has accumulated substantial life experience
and knows that life has a very large component of suffering.
Suffering is part of being human. At one time or another, we
all find ourselves in the presence of others' suffering in the
midst of our own. It is this inevitable life experience in all its
breadth and variety through which we suffer, endure, cope,
share, and continually grow. In this sense, we all have a great
commonality. If at the end of this reading you have a sense of
having reflected on our common human experience, my goal
will be reached. I do not have anything *to tell* you about suffering. All I can do is *reflect with you* about my own experience, knowing that we all share suffering as we do life.

Suffering: The Universal Experience

The common experience of suffering suggests the phrase "all
creation groans" from St. Paul's epistle to the Romans. The
words describe the universal and pervasive groaning of which
we are each a part. Our own individual groans, tears, and
cryings out in the night may be different from anyone else's,

but the phenomenon and experience permeate nature. We read recently about a terrible earthquake in Turkey where thousands of people were killed — the earth groaned. We hear of wars and invasions and conflicts — humanity groans. Distance from these events and our feelings of powerlessness and helplessness as global bystanders are a kind of suffering — we groan. St. Paul expressed our feelings and thoughts when he wrote (Rom. 8:18-23):

> I consider the sufferings of the present to be as nothing compared to the glory to be revealed in us. Indeed the whole created world eagerly awaits the revelation of the sons and daughters of God. Yes, we know that all creation groans and is in agony even until now. Not only that, but we ourselves, groan inwardly while we await the redemption of our bodies.

In some way each of us is suffering, even though it may be known only to ourselves. If there is anything in this world that is certain besides death and taxes, it is suffering. Yet, despite its universality, suffering is not an explanation for itself. It does not make sense in its own right.

The Why? of Suffering

But suffering is something that fairly cries out for explanation — it seems so unfair, so wrong. Suffering inevitably raises the question, why? Why me? Why me, Lord? Why this suffering? this persecution? this war? Suffering is like an irritant in the eye. It is an irritant in the world, an irritant in our own lives. It keeps making us aware of its presence, and forces us to look for its meaning.

Some people think that God is cruel, that he tortures and torments us. Religions have been built on the notion that God is a tormentor who somehow enjoys seeing us squirm in pain. Otherwise why does all this suffering go on? That is a dilemma for the theologically minded. Other people who are not theologically minded might say that life is absurd, and let us get on

with it. At best, suffering may be seen as an inevitable concom-
itant to change, growth and improvement; part of an evolution-
ary process. Yet even if we accept that understanding, suffering
is an experience that demands further explanation, a deeper
consideration of its meaning.

Is earthly groaning simply a cry of anguish? a painful out-
burst? a scream in the night that may or may not have an ear to
hear it? Or is earthly groaning a language, a very elaborate
language that needs understanding and interpretation as all language does?

What is suffering? Most simply, suffering is unwanted pain.
Its essence seems to be in that unwantedness. We do not like
it. We do not choose it. It is against our will. It is a personal
distress, a pain we know as misery. We know it as inescapable
and inevitable, something out of our control; something we are
not able to choose or not choose. It defies rejection. It forces
itself upon us, and also forces a response from us. In this sense,
suffering is a statement, a language, the opening of a dialogue.
It is an uncomfortable, unwanted companion that we must talk
to, respond to, think about and continually try to understand as
we live with it.

The How? of Suffering

There are many possible responses to suffering (other than our
legitimate attempts to relieve it). We might try to anesthetize
ourselves with alcohol or drugs; or distract ourselves with various amusements. Another common response to suffering is
denial, the stiff-upper-lip, grin-and-bear-it, put-up-with-it,
endure, and hang-on-as-best-you-can approach. (Meanwhile,
do not face it, or try to understand or relate to your suffering.)
Smile. Go forward as though nothing was happening. Personal
despair is another possible response — the despair of self-blame
and poor self-image. We suffer, so we must be awful. We think:
God does not love me anymore.

Among the many possible responses, each of us has our own
personal response which we tend to slip into more or less auto-
matically. We may respond with suffering to a broken heart,

betrayal, physical pain or fear of approaching old age. We may suffer confusion amidst the rapid restructuring of the Church when we become uncertain of our way because things are not as they used to be. These responses are understandable.

A response resembling despair is self-pity, the victim mentality. (See how I suffer; don't you feel sorry for me?) There are also many forms of magic relief. A common form today is faith healing. It is thought that with enough faith, the right prayers, or the right person bestowing a laying on of hands, suffering will end. It is believed that God may be used to relieve the personal distress of individuals. To me, that is a misuse of God. We sometimes see very discouraged and disillusioned people who feel that God does not like them or that their faith is not strong enough, because they were prayed over and nothing changed. In my view, these are some of the inappropriate responses to suffering.

It is also possible to face suffering with acceptance. Acceptance does not mean simply a stoic attitude expressed as: Well, here it is; I have to live with it; I have to go on. Acceptance means more. It means finding meaning or putting meaning into our experience prompted by that recurrent question that arises whenever some unwelcome experience or distress presents itself, why? Obviously we are not asking about cause and effect. We are asking: Why pain at all?

Why are we surrounded with all this suffering and agony? First, I would like to suggest that we consider suffering as an attention getter — it does break through our armor. When we are suffering, our pretenses tend to disappear. While we may display smiling faces and go on as if nothing of consequence is happening inside us, we *know* that something is happening. Eventually, we are forced to look at it. In this way, the suffering heightens our awareness.

Let us imagine for a moment, a world without suffering. I have a feeling that we would live on a very superficial level of awareness, and with considerable complacency. I am not sure that we would really develop the depth we are capable of as human beings if we did not have suffering. Think about your own experience. What kind of person do you seek out when you need to share some trouble? I suggest that it is a person who has suffered, someone who can relate to pain on an experiential level. Some of the meaning within suffering is its shattering of superficiality and deepening of character.

The When? of Suffering

Suffering is a very serious reminder of death. Suffering is often a herald of death. Much of our time and cultural energy are spent denying and disguising the reality of death.[1] The gospel message has much to tell us about death. It also has much to say about the denial of death. At one point, Jesus tells the disciples that he must go down to Jerusalem to suffer, die, and in three days rise again. The disciples tell him to stop his unpleasant talk. Yet, the Lord had a different kind of message. It had to do with the importance and meaning of suffering and death.

In one form or another we all live with an illusion that all is well, or soon will be. We delude ourselves into thinking that all of this turbulence will be laid to rest. For example, people will stop being greedy and we will have world peace. At some level, we think that there will be an end to war and persecution; that there will be no more suffering, hunger and famine. Technology will change things. So far it has not happened, and I say it is not going to happen.

As long as life experience reflects the effects of sin, we are going to be faced with the reality of universal suffering. Any time we are tempted to forget the reality and truth of the presence of sin in the world, we need just look around us. What is this inhumanity that we share with one another, much to our mutual pain and discomfort, except the effects of sin? If we want to live in the illusion that all is well though reality tells us otherwise, we have two basic choices of how to behave in the face of suffering. Either we can gloss over reality so that it looks good to us and we can continue to pretend that all is well, or we can oppose reality by denying, anesthetizing, or distracting ourselves in some way.

There once was a man who reaped a rich harvest. His grain filled his barns and he thanked God that he now had enough for his retirement without any more worries. He was going to just sit back and enjoy himself — no more suffering. All those barns of grain were his guarantee against suffering. Then someone told him he would die that night.

There is no getting around it. We have no this-world security. Insecurity is the state that we are all in. In the face of that insecurity, we all in some measure fool ourselves. Suffering reminds us that all is not well. The strength and assurance we think we have is not real. There is an element of illusion in it. It is certaninly not permanent. We are going to die. That realization is part of the meaning of suffering.

The Meaning within Death

When people suffer they tend to develop a kind of self-transcendent attitude. Suffering draws us outward and beyond ourselves to a meaning that transcends particular events. We are familiar with the experience of Viktor Frankl.[2] While in a concentration camp, he struggled to find meaning in his suffering. He found it in transcendent love, and he survived. His love to be authentic had to encompass all of humanity, including his own tormentors. That kind of search for meaning, being drawn out beyond our limited vision, is what suffering calls us to do.

C.S. Lewis says that pain is God's megaphone to arouse a deaf world.[3] Pain is a call to realize that we are living a mystery. We are indeed, according to St. Paul (Col. 1:24), filling up in our bodies what is lacking in the sufferings of Christ for the sake of his body, the Church. What is lacking is the completeness of the incorporation of all the rest of us into that one body. It is his mystical body that is continuing to suffer and to die and to be raised for our redemption. Suffering, for us, is the entry experience into the pascal mystery. Everyone will be drawn through this narrow gate to salvation. But not everyone will know what is happening to them. Some will embrace the

experience in faith and find its true meaning, entering joyfully
and willingly. Others will enter kicking and screaming, crying
out and revolting. But enter, everyone must.

The Mystery within Death

We have been speaking of a mystery. But just what is a mystery? What do we mean when we speak of one or another mystery of Christ's life? Mystery means experience. It is the
experience of Christ's life that we can share in mystically as
members of Christ's mystical body. We are baptized into his
life experiences. Everything that happens to us, everything we
go through, endure, all of our sufferings, our joys, our happiness and peace, all are part of this shared life. Our life is not
our own. Every experience we have is a shared experience, and
we will never know the meaning of anything that happens to us
in life until we understand that we are sharing life with someone
else. When we suffer, we do not have to offer it up. We can
directly identify with Christ and say: I am suffering in, with,
and through him who is suffering in and through and with me,
as a sign of his love.

This is not merely the suffering of many people who are
sharing a common misery and who lean on one another in order
to commiserate. This is much more than that. It is a mystical,
existential union with Christ who is continuing his pascal mystery through time and through us. When we are baptized into
that experience, something amazing happens to us. We are
transformed by our baptism. Our problem is to become and
remain aware of that truth. When we view our experience
through the eyes of faith, it transforms and changes the meaning
of our experience; it adds dimension. Faith will not take pain
away but it will add a dimension of meaning. There is joy and
consolation in that meaning. Joy and pain, suffering and meaning are present simultaneously. If we contemplate, and if we
have the faith to realize that the Lord is sharing our experience
with us, we can embrace it even as he is embracing us.

I have a story that I would like to share with you which I think illustrates what I mean by mystery. The California prison Alcatraz closed in 1963. For four years before that, I used to visit there every month or two with the chaplain. On my first visit, I met a prisoner in the yard serving thirty-five years for bank robbery and assault. He was a very bitter, angry and tough man. When I was leaving the prison, I told the warden that I had met Larry Trumblay.

"Oh, you're wasting your time with him, Father, that guy is one of the worst convicts we have in here," he said.

"How come, what do you mean?"

"Well, he's been here for about ten or twelve years and he's been involved in all sorts of riots and strikes. He has earned no time-off for good behavior."

I was impressed that I had met a very tough person in the yard that afternoon.

A couple of months later I was at Alcatraz again, and while I was talking to some men in the yard, Trumblay came walking by with a couple of other men.

I called over to him, "Hey, Trumblay, how are you doing?"

He stopped and looked at me and said, "Do you remember me?"

I said, "Yeah, I never forget my friends!"

He said, "Nobody ever talked to me like that before. Nobody ever called me their friend."

"Well, I consider you a friend. The last time I was here we talked and got along pretty well."

So he came over and we chatted and talked again. That was the beginning of a very profound friendship. Larry became my closest friend. A couple of years after we first met, he was thrown in the hole for six months for starting a riot in the dining room. One day I was visiting him in the hole and he said, "You know, you've been so good about visiting us out here, we're going to repay the visit when we get out."

I said, "If you come over to my room in San Francisco some-day dripping wet, forget it. I don't want to get involved."

He said, "No, when we get out of the hole here, we're going to go back to Church."

"Are you a Catholic?"

"Yes," he said.

I asked him how long it had been since he had gone to church. He told me it was about sixteen years. He did go back to mass and confession, became a mass server, and from that day on he changed his behavior completely. My friend Larry straightened himself out and over the next couple of years became, at least according to Alcatraz standards, what could be considered a model prisoner. During this time, we had a teasing fantasy that he would be at my ordination. I was planning to be ordained in 1965, and he was doing thirty-five years, with no time-off for good behavior — the notion was pretty far-fetched.

In 1962, I went to Toronto to study theology. On my way there, I stopped in Chicago and visited Larry's family. His mother knew the change that had come over him as a result of our friendship and she remarked that if I had only known Larry before, he might not have ended up at Alcatraz. I said that if I had known Larry before, we would have both been out there. In 1963, the prison was closed. Larry was transferred to Leavenworth. We continued to correspond and a number of amazing things began to happen. He was in a prison from which he could get parole. Because of the change that he had gone through he started to get his good-time reinstated. He had his sentence reduced one hundred, two hundred, three hundred days at a time. Eventually he got his sentence reduced by about one third. In 1964, he actually became technically eligible for parole. But at the hearing, he was turned down flat. The parole board reasoned that his adjustment to prison life had been too stormy and his crime too vicious to let him out.

In 1965, he applied for a parole again, and to everyone's amazement, it was granted. He was released on May 23, 1965. We got permission from the Attorney General of the United States for him to come out of his parole area and a week and a half later he flew to San Francisco for my ordination on June 5,

1965. He presented me with an alb crocheted for me in Alcatraz. He said it was "something to remember him and the boys by." It was one of the proudest moments of his life, and mine as well, as he sat with my family in the front row of St. Ignatius church. It had all happened through the most unexpected circumstances.

As we went through that ordination weekend, my parents and friends loved him. Everybody who met him was fascinated because he was so shy and laid back although he was ruggedly handsome. When that ordination weekend was over, he went back to Chicago. A week and a half later he was killed in an automobile accident.

Now that you know his story as I experienced it, I want to use it as an illustration of mystery. A Chicago paper ran the following obituary.

BANK ROBBER DIES IN CRASH ON S.W. SIDE
Car Leaves No Skid Marks, Police Say

Lawrence Trumblay, 37, who escaped from three shooting scrapes in his brief career in crime as a young man, was killed yesterday when his car struck an abutment at Cicero Avenue and 83d Street.

Trumblay, described as an unemployed laborer, was crushed behind the wheel of his auto. Police said there were no skid marks and no witnesses to the accident.

Suspect in Holdups

Trumblay, who was a suspect in numerous Chicago holdups and burglaries, was convicted and sentenced to 30 years in prison in 1953 for the $53,000 holdup of a branch of the National Bank and Trust Company in South Bend. A teller was wounded by a shotgun blast in the robbery.

Before that Trumblay survived two gun duels and a wound he said he suffered accidentally while snake hunting.

Joins Gang of Toughs

He made his start at 18 when he joined a gang of young toughs in the neighborhood of 18th and Morgan Streets. The gang was linked to several murders and holdups by police. One included the Indiana bank robbery.

Well, what the world knew about Larry Trumblay is in that short obituary. Yet we know him in a different way, don't we? Larry's life and death was much more than just, BANK ROBBER DIES IN CRASH ON SOUTHWEST SIDE. He was a real person, and a very saintly person at that. So what we see, hear and read is not necessarily the whole story.

Larry was a man who had suffered a great deal and yet found meaning in his suffering through a relationship and a friendship with me. I, too, found meaning in my life through Larry. We got very, very close to one another. However, if we try to explain his suffering in its own terms, we are left with only a headline. And the apparent meaning of the event of his death is all the meaning there is. If we choose to know in a different way through the eyes of faith and love, we can see beyond appearance and discover the greater meaning in any life experience. Each of our life stories can be told in both ways: the surface story of a newspaper article, and the spiritual story, the theological story, the story of the meaning of our lives.

Imagine what the Jerusalem *Times* on Easter morning would have said, THREE CRIMINALS EXECUTED ON CROSSES OUTSIDE THE CITY GATES. It would have reported the details as they occurred. Where would the meaning of that event be told: in a newspaper or in the stories of his friends?

Conclusion
Suffering, then, is kerygmatic rather than enigmatic. Suffering is not simply a puzzle, an enigma; it is a kerygma, an announcement. It calls attention to something beyond itself, namely, the living ongoing presence of Christ amidst all this groaning. Suffering is the birth pangs of the new creation, always struggling to be born while always being threatened by the destructive violence of sin and its effects. We must then ask with St. Paul (Rom. 6:1) whether we should make more suffering so that the presence of Christ may abound? Of course not. The attitude of the good samaritan, to reach out in compassion, mercy, generosity, to relieve the pain of neighbors, is the posture toward

suffering that we must remember. Christ was both the merciful healer and the innocent victim in this world. We minister to Christ when we relieve suffering even as we are experiencing Christ when we experience suffering. Remember when Christ described the scene of the last judgment. He identified himself with the victims of suffering and praised those who relieve it even when they do not recognize that he is the sufferer.

Suffering offers us an invitation to share in the loving creativity of God. He called Jesus his beloved son. Then God proved it by taking what appeared to be ultimate failure, rejection, and alienation, and making it into new life. God's act of love for us is to transform suffering and death, the consequences of sin, and make them the means of salvation, as he did in the life and death of Larry. There is joy and consolation in this knowledge. All the saints in heaven will certainly attest to that. St. Paul says (2 Cor. 1:4-7):

> He comforts us in all our afflictions and thus enables us to comfort those who are in trouble, with the same consolation we have received from him. As we have shared much in the suffering of Christ, so through Christ do we share abundantly in his consolation, If we are afflicted it is for your encouragement and salvation, and when we are consoled it is for your consolation, so that you may endure patiently the same sufferings we endure. Our hope for you is firm because we know that just as you share it in the suffering so you will share it in the consolation.

We Christians are not masochists. We are not somehow or another fascinated by suffering, nor do we enjoy pain. We are supreme realists. We face the truth of life which means the truth of the meaning of suffering beyond surface appearances. We accept the unavoidable suffering of life and we listen to God as he tells us what it means, having given us the example of his son. We are privileged to live out the paschal mystery through his continued redemptive presence in our time — through him, and with him, and in him.

Endnotes

1. *See* Ernest Becker, *Denial of Death* (New York: Free Press, 1973).
2. *See* Viktor Frankl, *Man's Search for Meaning: An introduction to logotherapy* (New York: Pocket Books, 1963).
3. *See* C.S. Lewis, M.A., *The Problem of Pain* (New York: Macmillan, 1962).

Happy Are You Who Mourn— The Ministry of Compassion

Thomas A. Kane

- Compassion • The Mystery of Suffering
- The Ministry of Compassion for Emotional Sufferers
- Approval of Selfishness • The Cross
- The Challenge to the Redemptive Value of Emotional Suffering
- Signals of Distress and Appeals for Help

Reverend Thomas A. Kane, Ph.D., D.P.S., international executive director of the House of Affirmation, is a priest of the Roman Catholic diocese of Worcester. He pursued his undergraduate studies at St. Edward's University, Austin, Texas; his graduate studies at National University of Mexico, Rutgers University, and St. Bonaventure University; and his post-graduate studies at Boston University and the University of Birmingham, England. As an educator and psychotherapist, Father Kane is a consultant to several Roman Catholic and Protestant groups. He is a frequent lecturer to academic and medical communities in the United States and Europe and a visiting scholar at Harvard University. Father Kane is a member of several professional organizations, serves on the board of directors of the National Guild of Catholic Psychiatrists, and is the author of several publications.

It is a cool morning on a remote island in Maine. I am staying at a family inn where there is complete quiet, interrupted only by the crackle of the wood in the big iron stove which echoes to the library, where the fireplace whispers its warm sounds.

I turn on the radio for the 7:00 a.m. news. The Bangor station communicates in passing: "Cardinal Medeiros is resting comfortably after his open heart surgery and his physicians predict he will be able to be back to a full schedule in a matter of weeks." Thank God, I tell myself, and ask Our Lady to keep him in her care.

Now on with the preparation of my talk for the Suffering Symposium — "Happy Are You Who Mourn" — with emphasis on the ministry of compassion. I feel free — no phones, no people with pressing needs, no demands but to complete this paper.

Compassion

Scripture invites the Christian to "be compassionate as your heavenly Father is compassionate." Matthew's version relates: "You must be perfect as your heavenly Father is perfect" (Matt. 5:48). How fortunate I was as a young man when my Brother Novice Master explained to us that in this scripture passage we could substitute the word "compassionate" for "perfect." Years later I read that scripture scholars tell us the same thing. Father Don Senior states: "Following Jesus in his ministry of compassion defines the meaning of being perfect as your heavenly Father is perfect."

As we read the Gospels and embrace the Christian life with a greater sense of integrity, we are stripped of all false idealism, naive romanticism, elite pietism, and condescending pity. Scripturally, compassion invites *reflective action.*

> If a man who was rich enough in this world's goods saw that one of his brothers was in need, but closed his heart to him, how could true love of God be living in him? My children, our love is not just words or mere talk, but something real and active (Luke 3:18).

The deepest emotions of Jesus appear to have been displayed when healing was brought about and introduced to a life event by a display of human compassion. The Levite and the priest, paragons of Jewish virtue, appeared neither to reflect nor to act. The Good Samaritan did both. "Which of these three, in your opinion, was neighbor to the man who fell in with the robbers?" Jesus' listeners responded, "The one who treated him with compassion." Jesus told his followers: "Then go and do the same."

The word "compassion" comes from the Latin *cum patior* meaning to suffer with, endure with, struggle with. To be compassionate we must partake of hunger, nakedness, loneliness and pain; and empathize with the ambiguity in the lives of our sisters and brothers in the human family.

In a sense, the English language meaning of "compassion," even keeping its richer Latin etymology in mind, is far too weak when we try to explain the compassion of Jesus. The Greek verb used in scriptural texts is *splagchnizomai* derived from the noun *splagcha* which means intestines, bowels, and describes inner anguish — that which is from the deep inward parts. The Greek verb means a deep gut reaction, a profound impulse felt both physically and emotionally.

In the Scriptures when Jesus displayed compassion, it came from the very center of His being. Jesus is the incarnation of the compassion of the heavenly Father. A fifteenth century mystic, Meister Eckhart, once wrote: "You may call God love; you may call God goodness; but the best name for God is Compassion." Father Brennan Manning asks us to reflect: What do the exalted names, Son of God, Second Person of the Blessed Trinity and Kyrios bestowed on Jesus by later ages, signify but that God was present in the Compassionate One, in a unique, extravagant and definite way.[1]

In Jesus' own compassion, the messianic age followed and became history. The new age of good news dawned. The followers of Jesus were to be recognized by their loving concern, their non-judgmental attitude, and their compassionate care of their brothers and sisters. "I tell you most solemnly insofar as you did this to one of these . . . least brothers of mine, you did it to me" (Matt. 25:40). Without glamour and with little notoriety, works of mercy, feeding the hungry, sheltering the homeless, visiting the sick and imprisoned, teaching youth, assertively correcting and bearing wrongs, ministering to the emotionally impoverished, washing dirty feet, and praying with people identified those who had taken His name to themselves, the Christians.

"The tea is on," my good friend called from the kitchen. I leave my warm library, my writing, and share tea with my caring friend.

"How is your writing going?"

"Fine," I say. "Maybe a bit too theoretical."

"Have you heard the news?"

"Oh yes, several hours ago while you were still sleeping."

"I am sorry about your Cardinal — he was a gentle man of love."

It was from this Iranian man, my friend, a Moslem, I learned that the early report was not accurate and that Cardinal Medeiros had died.

"But just a few hours ago I heard on the radio that he was progressing well." The stages of Kübler-Ross grief — shock — denial — anger — acceptance — all seemed to go through me very quickly.

There I was writing on a theme, Happy Are You Who Mourn, and the Cardinal died. He had been so supportive to the ministry of the House of Affirmation. Only a few weeks before I had been speaking with him. He had heavy burdens of office that day but took the time to say how he liked the name of our new chapel at our Boston Center — The Chapel of Our Lady of Mental Peace.

Words are difficult to write with Cardinal Humberto Medeiros' death in mind. He walked in the imitation of Christ . . . a man, a priest, who taught us much about the compassion of Christ. "Who do you say I am?" These haunting words of scripture are attractive yet fearful for each of us, but Humberto   Medeiros — without   superficiality,   without clicheism — made the words of scripture his guide to action in this life. ''I believe that nothing can happen that will outweigh the supreme advantage of knowing Christ Jesus my Lord . . . and I look on everything else as rubbish, if only I can have Christ'' (Phil. 2:8). Rest in peace my friend.

The Mystery of Suffering

Karol Wojtyla, before his election to the papacy, in a book titled *Sign of Contradiction,* tells us: ''In holy scripture we find magnificent books about human suffering; and many verses in them, especially those attributed to the just man Job, which could put new life into our meditation.''

When ''the hand of the Lord struck'' the chosen people (Job 19:21), it seemed like total calamity to them. The last of the davidic kings had been imprisoned; the country had been devastated; the priests and all the educated classes had been deported to Mesopotamia; and above all, Israel's glory and hope, the holy city and the temple of Zion, guarantee of Yahweh's presence and protection, had fallen. ''God has delivered me into the hands of evil-doers and put me at the mercy of the godless'' is Job's lament (Job 16:11), and in terrifying phrases he curses the day he was born (Job 3:1-9). Even the most faithful in Israel are assailed by doubts. Why? Why does God destroy his own work? ''How long is the oppressor to go on insulting your name, O God, and how long is the enemy to go on reviling you? . . . Remember, Lord: the enemy is insulting you; a godless people is reviling your name'' (Ps. 74(73), 10,18). ''O God, why do you reject us forever; why does your anger blaze against the sheep of your pasture?'' (Ps. 74(73), 1).

And God replies. His reply, the word of God that ''makes the earth fertile and never returns without making it yield fruit'' (Isa. 55:10-11), is the beginning of the new stage in the history of salvation. Salvation is born of suffering that is apparently meaningless. It was in his own suffering that Job found the Lord.

Part of the law of suffering is that it entails loneliness for humankind. This loneliness is not always evident, nor does it occur at every level of suffering. The limits of human endurance are not reached in every illness; but the closer the suffering gets to those limits, the more the sufferer has to endure the pain alone. Such loneliness can be seen in the story of the just man Job. And when loneliness becomes the occasion for man to meet God, the purifying dimension of suffering is experienced beyond the confines of this life. The story of Jesus Christ serves to introduce us to the purifying dimension of suffering which goes beyond the confines of this world. ''The Lord Himself came to free and strengthen man, renewing him inwardly and casting out that prince of this world (cf. John 12:31) who held him in the bondage of sin (John 8:34). For sin has diminished man, blocking his path to fulfillment.'' [2]

Christianity offers the most satisfactory explanation of suffering in a world that would otherwise turn away from the idea of a God who would allow agonizing diseases, concentration camps, miserable family situations, and every other kind of evil. Even for the Christian, suffering is ultimately a mystery. However, we do experience suffering's purifying effects whereby human beings are free to choose to purify themselves through compassionate solidarity with the rest of the human race.

The Ministry of Compassion for Emotional Sufferers

For fourteen years my ministry, as a priest and as a founder of the House of Affirmation, has kept me close to those who suffer emotional unrest. One thing I have observed is that many times people receive more understanding support from others if they experience a physical illness, or even alcoholism, than neurosis, depression or behavioral problems. Such difficulties make others so uncomfortable at times that everyone's suffering is compounded. If I were to have my choice, I would choose cancer a thousand times over the daily, heavy burden of a depressed person. I do not mean to give the impression that the people I have ministered to have not received understanding from their superiors, bishops, and family or friends. Many times they have. What I am saying is that to suffer from an emotional illness in American and European society is to suffer twice, that is the individual suffers from illness *and* from the misunderstanding and fears that surround emotional problems. In Western cultures, we tend to hold individuals totally responsible for their illness.

What motivates me in my ministry as a priest are the souls God has entrusted to our care at the House of Affirmation Centers — seven in this country and one in England. In this work, we are invited to participate in the compassion of Christ that purifies us as we share in the reception of the redemptive event. I see the presence of Jesus in emotional suffering. He reveals himself, his goodness, and his love to me in a very real way.

When I grow discouraged by fund-raising, balancing books, renewing staff contracts, the burdens of travel (responsibilities that are often far from my primary center of interest as a priest and as a psychotherapist), I am encouraged by the people we minister to at the House of Affirmation. Their pain reveals the suffering Jesus. Their healing echoes anew the resurrection of Jesus.

When I reflect upon suffering, I think of two contemporary teachings that I think add to the suffering of many persons. One comes from contemporary psychology and the other from contemporary spirituality.

Approval of Selfishness

In contemporary psychology there is approval of selfishness, looking out for Number One. In my book *The Healing Touch of Affirmation* published in 1976, I wrote about how frightened I get of the abundant self-hyphenated words — self-realization, self-actualization, self-fulfillment, self-acceptance, self-direction. Now I know that it is necessary to have proper love of self. This is both popularly and spiritually good.

Father Brennan Manning, in his reflective book, *A Stranger to Self-Hatred,* reminds us that in urging us to compassionate caring for others, Jesus invites us to compassionate care of ourselves. Years ago Carl Jung wrote:

> The acceptance of oneself is the essence of the whole moral problem and the epitome of a whole outlook on life. That I feed the hungry, that I forgive an insult, that I love my enemy in the name of Christ — all these are undoubtedly great virtues. What I do unto the least of my brethren, that I do unto Christ. But what if I should discover that the least amongst them all, the poorest of all the beggars, the most impudent of all the offenders, the very enemy himself — that these are within me, and that I myself stand in need of the alms of my own kindness — that I myself am the enemy who must be loved — what then? As a rule, the Christian's attitude is then reversed; there is no longer any question of love or long-suffering; we say to the brother within us 'Raca,' and condemn and rage against ourselves. We hide it from the world; we refuse to admit ever having met his least among the lowly in ourselves."[3]

In an effort to restore health to ego, to the self, contemporary psychotherapy has also enhanced and supported a contemporary malady: preoccupation with self. In the name of scientific honesty and candor, psychological theorizing about human nature has become a significant force in minimizing individual responsibility and concern for others. We see this lack of concern for others and over concern for self in many contemporary ways of living: materialism carried to an extreme, no room for the sick or retarded, little time for the elderly; efficiency at the expense of concern of persons. What is needed is balance. Proper love of self can be taught only if it is seen in relationship to concern for the common good, for the need of others, for social concerns, for community awareness.

Many people view vulnerability as a sign of weakness. Service to one's neighbor without profit is seen as superfluous in relation to celebrating self. "I am on my own." I believe egotism is also the root evil of the rugged individualism seen in many religious communities. Some new psychologists and psychiatrists are viewed as new messiahs. Weakness and vulnerability are not considered avenues of growth but too often human experiences diagnosed as illness. However, to me, psychology is useful only if it actually allows and invites us to have a proper love of self so that we may in turn love our neighbor with a greater sense of integrity and service.

The Cross

The cross of Jesus is always a scandal. It is always foolish. The glory of Jesus is his cross and his compassionate service to others in liberating them to joy of the love of God. Adult living is difficult work. The task of the adult life is to affirm others on the pilgrimage of growth and development which means at times accepting pain and ambiguity. The adult self grows into an acceptance of the real self— the wounded, the sinful and incomplete self—acceptance of a real love of self that by its nature seeks to be radiant in the affirming service and relationship with others.

The Challenge to the Redemptive Value of Emotional Suffering

The second contemporary teaching that adds to suffering comes from the theological opinion that mental and emotional illness are not redemptive sufferings. Francis MacNutt is the early exponent of this contemporary theory and the echoes of this teaching go on.[4]

Redemptive suffering is suffering that in some way has purpose and significance in God's plan of salvation. To the degree

that suffering has some purpose, it is more bearable.[5] Suffering
that is not redemptive is futile.

MacNutt's opinion has value in that neurotic and psychotic
people should not be complacent in their illnesses and resist
help; nor should they permit themselves to succumb to the
advantages of the "secondary gains." They should try everything to find relief and cure, especially through prayer and the
healing of memories.

But MacNutt's opinion can also be pernicious in its impli-
cation that psychotics and neurotics who cannot find cure are
somehow out of God's plan of life, existing in a spiritual limbo.
At the very least, such exclusion is disheartening; indeed,
MacNutt's opinion has caused many mentally and emotionally
ill people much anxiety. There is reason to believe that there
are psychological cripplings as irreversible as the loss or crip-
pling of physical limbs.

In my opinion, MacNutt's position is not theologically sound.
Nothing is outside God's redemptive plan, as if he is either
ignorant of such situations or powerless to change them; or not
loving enough to want to. God permits nothing to happen, not
even sin itself, without some plan to work it into the larger
economy of salvation.

MacNutt has expressed the opinion that from an objective
point of view depressed persons are living in a sinful state
because they lack hope, although on a subjective basis they are
not guilty for their hopelessness because their will power cannot
cope with their condition. This use of the concept of sin is too
broad; depression is an emotional state, not an action, and the
sufferer's will has not even yielded to it, any more than one
yields to a broken arm or leg. It is not a question of yielding to
a sinful action under pressure, which is objective sin, but suffering the existence of a condition. Moreover a depressed person
often continues to pray for help and to wish for relief. The
condition itself is not too dissimilar from experiences of the
dark night of the soul. St. Therese of Lisieux reported that she
could no longer say that she believed in God, but only that she
wished she could. St. Teresa of Avila reported the anguish of

depressed souls who could not believe in the possibility of their being saved, especially if they had been sinners earlier in life. Yet experiencing doubt can have profoundly beneficial spiritual effects, effects that purify the soul.

MacNutt has argued that a depressed person cannot work or relate to others, but this is equally true of many persons with organic illnesses. He has also argued that a depressed person cannot experience the inner joy and peace of a Christian, cannot believe in God's love, and cannot shake off a continual state of anxiety although Christ said we should not be anxious.

These observations are true at one level but not at another. At the level of feeling experience, they are accurate statements; at the level of spirit and faith experience, they can be completely wrong. A depressed or anxious person can have a real sense of God's love and care in faith even during severe feeling experiences of suffering. The anxiety the Lord refers to is not pathological anxiety but the more or less deliberate anxiety persons permit themselves out of pessimistic, petulant or rebellious attitudes.

Signals of Distress and Appeals for Help

Emotional illness is not meaningless suffering. It is a human signal of distress and an appeal for help that can lead to a process of healing and spiritual growth. In Jung's concept of psychological illness, the neuroses and psychoses are manifestations of the struggles of a crippled and thwarted personality to grow toward maturity. In the struggle, the deeper spiritual needs are exposed. The pain of exposure is not meaningless; it is the pain of fear, shame, and helplessness as persons are pressed by interior needs to face themselves as they really are. With the help of others and the grace of God, these persons can learn to be self-affirming and reach self-acceptance. The ministering of caring people is itself an ingredient that cures the spirit as it enters into experiential awareness through sharing and exploring with another. Also the sense of prayers answered puts flesh on an often debilitated faith.

It may happen that a total cure is not possible; that scars will remain for a lifetime. But a person can live with these scars and perhaps grow more because of them. A person who cannot feel love and affection can come to understand the cause of this disability and still reach out to help others, in a care-full thoughtful way. It is even possible that the essence of love rooted in the spirit grows stronger when loving acts are more willed than felt. In this way the essence of virtue grows, especially faith, hope, and love. "I wish I could believe; I wish I could trust; I wish I could love" can be statements that signal deeper spiritual goodness than acts that flow from affective levels.

Our mourning, our sorrow, can in its own mysterious way reveal our neighbor. Suffering that reveals Christ to us purifies our restless hearts, eases our present deprivations, moves us to hope for a future contentment here on earth and in the life to come. We can say that we, who are the happy, mourn because we live with hope and joy in Christ. Alleluia, Alleluia. More important than mourning, more important than sorrow, is our joy and hope in Christian community and compassion on earth and the promise of future glory. "So also now indeed you have sorrow, but I will see you again and your heart shall rejoice; and your joy no man shall take from you" (John 16:22).

Conclusion
Dietrich van Hilderbrand in his book *Transformation in Christ* offers a rich insight into the reality of the Christian life. He reminds us that in the Beatitudes (Matt . 5:3-11), our Lord indicates the eminent value of the qualities praised by coupling them with rich, heavenly rewards. It is easier, however, to understand, "happy are the merciful"; "happy are the peacemakers"; and "happy are the pure of heart" than it is to respond to "happy are you who mourn." Why should they who mourn be happy?

Our Lord is reminding us that this "valley of tears" is not all there is. All of us who suffer on earth — the oppressed, the disinherited, the sick and the poor, the lonely — all of us who experience personal suffering in our lives must also remember daily our example in Christ and his eternal promise to us.

Endnotes

1. Brennan Manning, T.O.R., *Stranger to Self-Hatred* (Denville, N.J.: Dimension Books, 1982).
2. Walter M. Abbott, S.J., ed. "Gaudium et Spes," *The Documents of Vatican II* (New York: Guild Press, 1966), p. 211.
3. C.G. Jung, *Modern Man In Search of a Soul* (New York: Harcourt, Brace and World Harvest Books, 1933), p. 235.
4. Francis MacNutt, *Healing* (New York: Bantam Books), pp. 163–65.
5. For a more developed essay on this subject, *see* Michael Stock, O.P., "Meaning in Mental and Emotional Suffering," *Bulletin of National Guild of Catholic Psychiatrists,* vol. 23 (1977): 49–53.

Suffering: Masochism Versus Sanctity

Richard J. Gilmartin

- Holiness and Pain; Sanctity and Suffering
- Masochism • Sanctity
- The Bias of Sainthood
- Heroic Witness and Religious Vision

Richard J. Gilmartin, Ph.D., is director of the House of Affirmation in Whitinsville, Massachusetts, and an associate professor of counseling psychology at Worcester State College and Anna Maria College. He pursued his graduate education at Fordham University, New York University, and St. John's University, and received his doctoral degree from Kensington University, Los Angeles. Before joining the staff of the House of Affirmation he was psychological counselor at Worcester State College; director of counseling and instructor in the Graduate School at Assumption College, Worcester; chairperson of the psychology department at St. Francis College in Brooklyn; and supervising psychologist at the Religious Consultation Center of the diocese of Brooklyn.

My usual approach to topics such as suffering is to focus on the psychological aspects of the issues and leave the theological/ spiritual aspects to the theologians. Not being trained in theology, I believe this is a legitimate approach. But now I am wearying of Freudian inquests of religious issues. While I acknowledge my lack of theological expertise, I must also profess my Christianity. I do not lack opinions on religious issues. I am therefore writing as a psychologist who professes Christian faith and who has worked therapeutically with religious professionals for over sixteen years. I am not a professional theologian, but I want to include the religious and psychological in our consideration of the dimensions of masochism and sanctity.

Holiness and Pain; Sanctity and Suffering

In the psychological literature, there is no lack of speculation on the nature of the religious experience. For the most part in the past, when psychology and religion were put together, there was a tendency for one to be served at the expense of the other. Either the religious experience was seen as a sublimated attempt to resolve primitive conflicts, or psychology was used to defend religious/moral positions in an apologetic endeavor. Both approaches failed to do justice to either psychology or religion.

Today, although many psychologists approach the religious experience with suspicion most, at least in theory, would recognize that the religious experience has a legitimacy that is not reducible to psychopathology. Without doubt, much religious experience is a manifestation of the pathological. One need only to think of the extreme religious practices of the flagellantes; some of the re-enactments of the crucifixion; the sadistic behavior of the Inquisition; or the story of the saint who used to hide herself in the oven whenever visitors came to the convent. With the possible exception of war, we know there is no area of human experience that provides the opportunity for pathology to parade as virtue as does religion. But at the same time, it is unwarranted to leap from the fact that some virtue can be pathognomic to the conclusion that all virtue, at best, is sublimated psychopathology. Rather it is our conviction that the religious experience can stand by itself as a legitimate manifestation of the human experience and that it is not reducible to an intrapsychic illusion.

As I mentioned earlier, most psychologists would agree theoretically with our assertions about religious experience. Religion is not the universal neurosis, the convenient crutch for the ailing psyche, the institutionalized myth which must be transcended for wholeness to be achieved. At the same time, we must acknowledge that neurosis can be manifested and perpetuated in religious practice. In outward manifestations, sanctity also invites dichotomous views. Sanctity can be a genuine personal holiness or an expression of pathology, which is never easy to judge. Either is possible. On the one hand, to see the sacrifice of someone like Maximilian Kolbe as the manifestation of an unconscious self-destructive wish would be to miss the significance of his actions. On the other hand, it would be naive to believe that self-destructiveness does not happen. Martyrdom and other heroic deaths can be acted-out suicidal wishes.

It is unquestionably true to say that suffering is a part of holiness. It is unquestionably naive to assert that *all* suffering is holiness. But to distinguish between suffering that is a manifestation of the human condition and/or a striving toward the Holy, and suffering that is an expression of masochistic impulses is a difficult task. It is to this task that we address ourselves.

Masochism

Masochism is one of those not-uncommon but not-well-understood phenomena of human behavior. In its simplest form, it is one of the sexual "deviations," wherein one achieves sexual (genital) gratification from being maltreated, either by a partner

or by oneself. Masochism was first described in the mid-1800s
by the Austrian novelist Leopold von Sacher-Masoch. Masochism is the under-coin of sadism, and they are usually coupled
as sadomasochism.

But masochism is a very complex phenomenon, multimoti-
vated, and expressed in a variety of ways, most of which are
nongenital. However, all its manifestations have the common
component of a need to suffer.

We all know what masochism is and that to some degree it
may be in all of us. Why that is, is difficult to answer. There
are many theories to explain masochism and each of the theories has some truth. The multiplicity of theories reflects the
multiple causations of this single phenomenon.

Sigmund Freud (1856–1939) addressed the problem of
masochism in his later writings. His attempt to explain all
human behavior on the basis of a single motivating dynamic,
the pleasure principle (eros), floundered as he tried to explain
this apparently nonpleasurable compulsion. To account for the
self-injury and self-destructive behavior he observed, he pos-
tulated a death instinct (thanatos), which operated with eros as
the dual dynamic in human behavior.

Some subsequent psychoanalytic thinkers tend to reject a
death instinct and account for masochism as a defense against
sadism. Within the masochist are hostile, sadistic impulses
which the masochist denies. This denial is reinforced by a
retreat into the opposite, that is, masochism. Others see
masochism as hostility that gets directed inward and manifested
in self-depreciating and self-punitive behavior. Still others see
it as a manifestation of deep-seated feelings of guilt, and the
masochism as an attempt at atonement.

Outside the psychoanalytic school of thought, theories
abound to explain masochism. Learning theorists view it as a
form of conditioning. In experiments with laboratory cats,

where the cats are given a mild electrical shock either shortly before or during feeding, a connection gets built between the pain and pleasure in such a way that the pain itself becomes pleasurable. In such experiments the cats pursue the electrical shocks even when there is no food forthcoming. The shocks, or suffering, become pleasurable ends in themselves.

In a different direction, Karen Horney (1885 – 1952) saw masochism as part of personal character structure, a person's characteristic way of coping with life. For her, masochism is goal-oriented behavior, the goal actually being the avoidance of suffering. Paradoxically, suffering is used to avoid suffering. The suffering I create for myself is always less painful than anticipated suffering. By being in personal pain, albeit self-created, I am dispensed from taking responsibility for myself and my life and I thereby avoid anticipated suffering.

Wilhelm Reich (1897 – 1957) also saw masochism as part of character structure. But rather than experiencing pain as pleasure, the masochist experiences pleasure as pain and therefore avoids pleasure. From this point of view, pain is not being sought, but rather pleasure is being avoided. The issue is one of not being able to accept love. For the masochist, love is loaded with fear and anticipated pain. The masochist has an intense desire for love, but this is outweighed by the fear of love. Therefore love is avoided in all its manifestations. Masochists would rather have someone beat them than love them. Beating is less painful than love for a masochist.

Another interesting theoretical approach is that of Sandor Rado (1890 –   ) who calls masochism "pain-dependent behavior." He sees it as a form of expiatory behavior arising from an intense fear of guilt. Guilt is painful, but the fear of guilt is much more painful and a much more powerful control on behavior than guilt itself. According to Rado, for the masochist the fear of guilt is so great that punishment is sought in advance so that the forbidden pleasurable desires can then be gratified and guilt avoided. It is as if one satisfies the talion law by banking a reserve of punishment that then allows a forbidden indulgence, by-passing the guilt for the transgression. As a result, the masochistic circle of punishment and indulgence becomes established.

There are other theories, but we have shown the complexity of masochistic behavior. To summarize briefly, masochism is a pathology in which pain and suffering are necessary characteristics of an individual's lifestyle. Suffering is used as a neurotic adaptation to life. By maintaining a state of pain and suffering the greater pain of guilt and responsibility, the price of coping with life, is avoided.

By way of illustration, in the process of therapy if, after a reasonable period of time, I feel that nothing is changing in my client and that, even though we may be talking about significant life issues, I do not see any improvement or change taking place, my first question would be: Is there something inside me, in my personality, or in my unconscious reactions to the client, that prevents the person from growing? If, after consultation with a colleague, I cannot discover anything, my second question would be: Is there something diagnostic that I am missing? The first thing I would look for would be alcoholism, since alcoholics do not get better in traditional forms of psychotherapy. The second thing I would look for would be masochism. Not that the masochist cannot be helped in psychotherapy, but the problem has to be confronted and dealt with because the client has a lot invested in not giving up the pain and suffering. Masochists will defeat therapy if one lets them.

Masochists unconsciously seek out painful situations and experiences. We may speak of accident proneness, fear of success, self-defeating behavior or being the perennial victim. Or we may see such behavior as holiness or sanctity. And that is my prime concern here — the connection between holiness and pain, and sanctity and suffering.

Obviously a penitential, self-sacrificing, mortification-valuing lifestyle offers a haven for the masochist. Masochists will flourish in a harsh environment, and the more severe the suffering the more they will like it. But most of us would agree that this has little to do with real holiness and, even though in particular cases it may be difficult to distinguish masochism from holiness, the two are not the same. What I would like to do is to attempt to establish some criteria for distinguishing masochism from holiness.

Sanctity

What does it mean "to be a saint"? The word "saint" has wide popular usage which is not much help in understanding what being a "saint" means. We hear such expressions (even by a recent U.S. president) as "my mother was a saint," or a self-deprecating "I'm no saint . . . but." I remember at the end of my high school dances, the band invariably played "When the Saints Go Marching In." In his obituary, Buckminster Fuller was called "a secular saint." We pray to, or through, saints; when we lose something we pray to St. Anthony; if we cannot find it we pray to St. Jude. We name cities, towns, holidays, and athletic teams after saints. Mother Theresa of Calcutta is described as a "living saint." But, what does that mean? What does this "being a saint" mean?

I wanted to see how theologians define sanctity in order to react to it as a psychologist. Since sainthood and Roman Catholicism are inextricably linked together, I asked a theologian friend for the name of a good compendium of Catholic theology. He recommended Richard McBrien's two volume work entitled *Catholicism.*[1] Remarkably, there is not a single index reference to "saint" or "sanctity." I went to the recent *An American Catholic Catechism.*[2] Again, not a single reference to "saint." There is one reference to "sanctification" and that has to do with the charism a man receives at ordination. Now, one could argue that the whole intent of theology is toward making saints and therefore it would not be given a separate index reference. But, I found twenty-two references to ''salvation'' and that, as much as sanctity, is a major intent of theology. There is a chapter on "Christian spirituality," but nothing on being a saint. I found what it means to be a mystic, but not what it means to be a saint.

I went on to peruse other books in theology and found, remarkably, that there is very little written on what a saint is. I read about the difference between *latria* and *dulia*, the worship of God and the veneration of saints. The process of canonization is described in detail, but an understanding of the juridical process of canonization is of little help in gaining insight into the saintly personality.

The current process of canonization within the Church has become so intertwined with the miraculous that the intrinsic value of saintly personhood has become obscured. Even though the moral witness of the saint's life is necessary for canonization, the determinative factor in the canonization procedure is still the miraculous. Nothing about what a saint is.

I came across two quite remarkable, although very different, little books that were helpful in understanding the meaning of sanctity. One was Jacques Douillet's *What Is a Saint* [3] and the other Lawrence Cunningham's *The Meaning of Saints*.[4] Both were quite stimulating in helping to think through what a saint is.

The Bias of Sainthood

It is an interesting experience to study the list of saints, especially those who were actually canonized, that is, those who come after the twelfth century when Pope Alexander III reserved the right of canonization to the papacy. Certain peculiarities stand out. First, the list is almost completely made up of clerical or religious professionals. (There are a token few lay people.) This may be partly due to the fact that it is generally the religious orders that have the time and means to finance the canonization process. The problem is that while saints are to be universal models, the majority of the Church is neither clerical nor professional religious. The lifestyle of the canonized saint is not that of most Christians. The list of saints suggests a definite bias.

Other prejudices are also evident. Although, unlike other areas of the Church, women are adequately represented on the list of saints, the way they are classified and presented is interesting. Women are classified as either virgins or non-virgins. In fact, in the category "non-virgins and widows" not one male is found; the list is entirely composed of females. Not even St. Augustine of Hippo made the category for which, if one believes his *Confessions,* he was certainly eligible. There is a very narrow view of womanhood being perpetuated by the list of saints.

Another observation. No one would question that sanctity can exist outside the bounds of the Roman Catholic Church. But this is not reflected in the calendar of saints. The criterion of doctrinal orthodoxy precludes the possibility of canonization to anyone other than the strictly orthodox. What a phenomenal gesture toward ecumenism it would be if someone like Deitrich Bonhoffer received official recognition from the Church for the sanctity of his life and martyrdom. What a powerful statement that would be that holiness can be achieved without doctrinal conformity; that heroic sanctity can exist outside the parameters of Roman Catholicism; that the call to sanctity is a universal one; that holiness embraces a Bonhoffer, as well as a Maximilian Kolbe; that an Albert Schweitzer or a Ghandi can embody holiness and be an inspiration and model for all of us. Indeed, one gets the impression that canonization has been used to promote doctrinal and spiritual conformity rather than provide models of holiness for inspiration and emulation.

The search for what it means to be a saint goes beyond looking at the official saints of the Church. Maybe it is necessary for us to distinguish between the Saint and the saint. "Saint" is not synonymous with miracle worker. We tend not to think

of Mother Theresa as a saint because she has never performed
miracles, nor did Tom Dooley nor Albert Schweitzer, nor Pope
John XXIII nor Dag Hammarskjöld.

What is a saint? I offer the definition of Lawrence
Cunningham.
> A saint is a person so grasped by a religious vision that it
> becomes central to her or his life in a way that radically
> changes the person and leads others to glimpse the value of
> that vision.[5]

Read the words again: "grasped by a religious vision." As
William James writes in *The Varieties of Religious Experience,*
in every saint there is a conversion, a transformation, that
effects a new direction in life.[6] This conversion can be a sudden
Road-to-Damascus experience, as we see in the life of St. Paul,
St. Francis of Assisi, and St. Ignatius of Loyola. Thomas Merton describes his experience:
> In Louisville, at the corner of Fourth and Walnut, in the
> center of the shopping district, I was suddenly overwhelmed
> with the realization that I loved all these people, that they
> were mine, and I theirs, that we could not be alien to one
> another even though we were total strangers. It was like
> waking from a dream of separateness, of spurious self-iso-
> lation in a special world, the monastic world of renunciation
> and supposed holiness.[7]

Or it can be a slow and gradual transformation as we see in the
life of St. Theresa of Lisieux. Dag Hammarskjöld describes
his experience:
> I don't know Who — or what — put the question. I don't
> know when it was put. I don't even remember answering.
> But at some moment I did answer "Yes" to Someone — or
> something — and from that hour I was certain that existence
> is meaningful and that, therefore, my life, in self-surrender,
> had a goal.[8]

These transformative experiences frequently do not represent the beginning of a person's spiritual life, but more likely are the "moment of insight" after a life lived as a religious person.

What this "conversion" invariably does though is to decrease ego-centeredness and to open the person to what James calls the "feeling of being in a wider life." Asceticism, in the form of self-denial, flows from this conversion, as a natural consequence of it, rather than leading to it. As the saintly open to the wider vision of their existence, they naturally and willingly sacrifice themselves to it. This religious vision becomes consuming and the role of self takes on a new meaning.

This transformation is analogous to what Reinhold Niebuhr is talking about when, in *The Children of Light and the Children of Darkness,* he describes ultimate evil:

> Evil is always the assertion of some self-interest without regard to the whole, whether the whole be conceived as the immediate community, or the total community of mankind, or the total order of the world. The good is, on the other hand, always the harmony of the whole on various levels. Devotion to a subordinate and premature "whole" such as the nation, may of course become evil, viewed from the perspective of a larger whole, such as the community of mankind. The "children of light" may be thus defined as those who seek to bring self-interest under the discipline of a more universal law and in harmony with a more universal good.[9]

In this transformation, the religious vision becomes central. Asceticism arises not from choice, but from self-forgetfulness. St. Vincent de Paul was not a saint because he was charitable, but rather he was charitable because he was a saint.

It is at this very point where the differentiation between the pathological personality and the saint becomes most evident, but also most difficult to distinguish. It is in ascetical practices and self-abnegation that the masochistic personality feeds and nurtures itself. In the saint the self-forgetfulness arises out of the consumption of the religious vision. In the saint, the asceticism serves the saintly personality, while in the masochist the self-abnegation, suffering, and pain are ends in themselves, or serve non-saintly goals. This distinction is not an easy one to make, but in the saints one feels a sense of joy and a sense of gift in receiving what life offers; in the masochists one senses the painful burden that life is for them.

It should be noted, though, that sanctity is no guarantee against neurosis, nor vice versa. Neurotics (including masochists) can be saints too, as can unpleasant or unattractive personalities. Think of the virulent anti-semitism of St. Vincent Ferrer or the suspicious self-mutilation of St. Rose of Lima. Sanctity is not just for the whole and the healthy.

Hear the words of Lawrence Cunningham again: The saint *"leads others to glimpse the value of that vision."* The saint's holiness is always a sign of value for others. To use Paul Tillich's words, the saint is always a "sign-event" for others, maybe only a few others or maybe many others, but there is always an other. The saint may be a universal sign, or limited to historical or social circumstances. The sign can be of the perennial significance of certain religious values, such as faith, hope, love, or poverty; or it may signify a new way of enfleshing an ideal, such as the Beatitudes. In a particular historical-cultural circumstance, the brothers Berrigan gave new meaning to love of neighbor. Dag Hammarskjöld underwent a new martyrdom in the cause of peace.

The saint teaches others the perennial value of the religious vision of life and/or new and different ways of living out those values. In a Christian sense, the saint reincarnates gospel values and shows us new ways of enfleshing those values.

Frequently saints are at odds with the institutions and established ways of doing things and their signal value may not be evident for years to come. Recently an item in the newspapers described a pilgrimage of those in the anti-nuclear movement to the grave of Franz Jagerstatter, a farmer and church sexton in his native Austria. Poor, uneducated, father of three children, Jagerstatter was a deeply pious Catholic and, out of his faith, a committed pacifist. Because of his conviction, he refused to serve in the Nazi army. He was vilified in his pro-German village; even his bishop tried to convince him that to serve in the Army was his Christian duty. Franz Jagerstatter held to his conviction. He was imprisoned, tortured, and beheaded in a Gestapo prison on August 9, 1943, and subsequently buried in an obscure grave in his village graveyard. Two years to the day of his death, August 9, 1945, the first atomic bomb was dropped on Japan.

Franz Jagerstatter will probably never be canonized. But he has become a sign-event of the peacemaker, an enfleshment of a gospel value in a life that stands in sharp contrast to an event two years after his death.

Cunningham has written:

> The saints are at the very cutting edge of the Church; they are the harbingers and the prophets of what the Church needs to be and needs to do in a given historical moment. They are the avant-garde who testify to the needs of the time. At the same time, they testify to the possibility of sanctity in a given epoch, a sanctity germane to their time and an example that stands historically as an enriching paradigm for the future.[10]

Some saints are certified through the process of canonization and in this sense they offer the hope of salvation. But more than this, the official and unofficial saints show forth new ways of being holy, or Christian, as well as the value of the old. The saint shows what it means to be truly religious. Every person is called to be a saint and, in response, each builds up the communion of community in individual and unique ways.

Heroic Witness and Religious Vision

There are saints all around us, the majority of whom will never be certified. One thinks of Ghandi, Bonhoffer, Kolbe, Jagerstatter, Martin Luther King, Jr., Thomas Merton, Simone Weil,

Albert Schweitzer, Pope John XXIII, Dorothy Day, Peter Maurin, Dag Hammarskjöld, and countless others who show us new ways to live the old values. There are the pacifists, the feminists, the liberationists who work to enflesh the beatitudes of peace, justice, and human dignity in our time.

To come full circle, the masochist and the saint represent polarities. They stand in opposition to each other. The masochists in their repression and denial of their humanity and in their embrace of pain and suffering as an avoidance of the human condition, stand in sharp contrast to the saints who, transcending self in the pursuit of the religious vision, seek to reincarnate the message of love.

But suffering is in the lives of all of us. There is the human suffering of disease, death, loss and failure. There is the spiritual suffering of pitting our life against hostile environments. There are saints providing heroic witness in the Gulags of Russia and in Argentinian prisons. But there is also heroic witness in the more commonplace environments of indifference, of smug middle-class materialism, of racism. More often than not sanctity is an individual effort against a majority consensus in the pursuit of a religious vision.

There is also boredom and everydayness and sheer drudgery in the day-to-day pursuit of a vision that may be the greatest suffering of all. The "heroic moment" in the life of the saint is easily seen. The day-to-day drudgery of the saint's routine life is easily forgotten. Few of us are called to dramatic martyrdom. Most of us are called to routine everydayness, not heroic moments. But within our lifetime of sameness, we must make the continuous effort to renew ourselves in the pursuit of our vision. This also may cause great suffering.

The Desert Fathers spoke of the "noon-day devil" as the source of greatest suffering. Analagous to life, the "noon-day devil" is the spirit of discouragement, doubt, ennui and boredom that strikes between the enthusiasm and fervor of morning, and the refreshment of sleep in the evening. This mundane, daily suffering may be the most difficult to deal with. But the call to holiness, the call to enflesh the Gospel today, involves a continuous facing of the "noon-day devil" and a repeated triumphing over it in the pursuit of our individual visions.

Endnotes

1. *See* Richard McBrien, *Catholicism* (Minneapolis: Winston Press, 1980).

2. *See* George J. Dyer, *An American Catholic Catechism*, (New York: Seabury Press, 1975).

3. *See* Jacques Douillet, *What Is a Saint* (New York: Hawthorn Books, 1958).

4. *See* Lawrence Cunningham, *The Meaning of Saints* (New York: Harper and Row, 1980).

5. Ibid., p. 65.

6. William James, *The Varieties of Religious Experience* (New York: Mentor Press, 1958), p. 42.

7. Thomas Merton, *Conjectures of a Guilty Bystander* (Garden City, N.Y.: Doubleday, 1966), p. 96.

8. Dag Hammarskjöld, *Markings* (New York: Alfred A. Knopf, 1964), p. 124.

9. Reinhold Niebuhr, *The Children of Light and the Children of Darkness* (New York: Charles Scribner's Sons, 1953).

10. Cunningham, p. 79.

Re/Membering — Members of Myself

Rita D'Andrea

- Child • Mother • Therapist
- The Oppressed Ones • The Seer
- The Accommodator • The Conformer
- The Projector

Rita Linda D'Andrea, M.A. (cand.), is a full-time dance and art therapist at the House of Affirmation in Montara, California. She holds Bachelor's degrees in physiological psychology from Indiana University of Pennsylvania, and in education from Christian Brothers College in Memphis. Ms. D'Andrea trained in dance therapy at Antioch University in San Francisco, and is a professional dancer, mime, poet, and choreographer concerned with women's issues and social activism. Her workshops include non-verbal communication, group process, and community building. In addition, she works with individuals and groups employing movement, imagery and metaphor as means to psychological insight and transformation.

Introduction

The choreopoem "Re/Membering" is a composite of dance, mime, poetry, imagery and dramatic readings. The excerpts from "Re/Membering" that follow are offered as model — as metaphor — in the comprehension of suffering. Each creative act takes raw material to transformation — word to poem, shadow-move to dance, clay to vessel. The process of creating is a tension — often intense — that permeates the creator and precludes rest until resolution/meaning is found. A process not unlike suffering which can be both raw material and process of transformation. That which we accept as cause of suffering (raw material) potentially holds within it beauty and clarity. Mourning, for example, encases the love for the lost one, the depth of which might be unclear until it is perceived through grief.

The dis-ease of the process of suffering moves us and fuels us toward the moment of resolution. That moment will manifest in different ways, perhaps as insight or acceptance, but most important something within us will have altered. We are required only to permit the transformation, to join with the suffering not as its victim but as its partner — its re-creator.

An Exercise:
Re/membering members of myself

   Please, come be with me a bit. Take a few minutes after reading this and be with me, not with the fine sense of cognition but with the sense of deepest knowing. If you will, image with me. That could mean visualizing, remembering, pretending.

   Close your eyes. Notice your breathing. Stay there a few moments. Then image, remember, pretend there is a box on your lap — any kind you like, cardboard, wood, whatever. I'd like you to reach in and pull out the first item, which is a knife. This is the knife that shapes wood; this is the knife that shapes clay; this is the knife that creates forms out of formlessness. The name of the knife is suffering. Reach in again; there is a match. Strike it, and hold the flame before you — the flame that reduces massive trees to ash; the flame that takes chill to warmth; the flame that takes dark to light; the flame that consumes and is called suffering. Reach in again. This time there is a book. The title of the book is Suffering. *Its pages are filled with characters. Some of them will look and feel very familiar, among them: the child, the projector, the dreamer, the oppressed ones. But there are others, those who have been transformed through suffering.*

   Please, be gentle with analysis. Try not to discern but merely relate. Try not to understand but feel and recognize the characters who live within you.

   Come with me, now. Take a few minutes. Close your eyes. Notice your breathing . . .

Child

Yellow slicker kicks a can
    absently
Force within —
    withheld
Just taps the can
    lightly

Piggy banker counts the dimes
    urgently
Tears within —
    withheld
Recounts the dimes
    nightly

Baby-keeper rocks the girl
    tenderly
Envying
    withheld
Then pats her cheek
    lightly

Mama's angel smiles for her
    earnestly
Rage within
    withheld
Then lives his life so
    rightly
Till he implodes
    unsightly

Mother

Elizabeth, it's been a year.
I walk this room and
   empty, it chills me.
I touch this crib and
   empty, it burns my hand.
My arms still ache with longing and
   I wonder if I'll ever heal.

It rained so many days last year,
   grey after grey
That I forgot that rain is
   supposed to erase the clouds.
I cried so many days last year,
   day after day
That I forgot that tears are supposed
   to erase pain.
Baby girl, I cling to those who are left to
   me.
I redo this agony every time one of them leaves
   for longer than a moment.
Elizabeth, we would have loved each other.
   I gave you to death —
      not willingly.

Therapist

Yes I see, yes, I hear you, and
   still I withdraw in silence.
How can I tell you, how can I find a way
   through your anguish to tell you
that suffering can melt into meaning.
   The pain can yield to meaning.
How can I convince you, that
   I will partner you.
I won't leave you alone there.
   No, I can see in your eyes
and in your body, and in your breath,
   you're not ready to hear.
Please don't go.

It is quite a different pain to
   cry tears for another.
The blade of that knife
   slashes and gouges
rather than merely
   stabs.
Twice the bleeding.
   Twice the grieving.
Once from the hand that reaches forth
   and contacts only air—
Once from the hand that reaches forth
   to offer a comfort he cannot bear.

The Oppressed Ones

I am the daughter of Lebanon
I tend my maimed —
I suffer my dead —
I ask you —
    "What meaning has all this?"

I am son of Nicaragua
Protector of my people.
Defender of our ways —
I ask you —
    "What meaning has all this?"

I am mother of Ireland and
I just watched my son die.
Die on a street littered with
    rhetoric and bullets.
Die because you want their rule —
Die because you don't.
Die because I find my God
    in this house.
Die because you find yours
    in this one.
I demand of all of you —
    "What meaning has all this?"
And why in the name of God
    do we permit it to continue?

The Seer

'68 Wonderings — '68 Wanderings

Now, why is it so sunny?
This makes absolutely no sense.
Funerals should not be skyscraped with sun.
         And where's the crowd?
Where are those who claim love of us?
Should they not be here to touch our hand,
meet our grieving tears?
Must I, draped black, mourning veiled,
dance this dirge alone?
So be it then.
         The hearse proceeds before my memory —
stained eyes. Back to the moment — no —
there was no moment of your conception.
You evolved from many seeds and
fertile tendings. You grew within me
nurtured by 3 a.m. strategy meetings,
Abraham, Martin, John, Bobby, and the endless
women who marched, and prayed. Your
birth was not a moment but a process.
We were never separated. We are one
at this moment, as we were then.
         Oh, now the rain comes.
It beats on the grave canopy
like the endless beating in my mind.
The torturous beats of beliefs that
you could live and grow despite poverty
of soul and the neglect into which you were born.

Oh, now the tears come.
The earth has opened. The agonizing
gasp of reality, of "economy" of greed
prepares to embed you.
Dream of peace, we bury you.
Belief in peace, we sing your eulogy.
Who can resurrect you?

The Accommodator

Some of us are pleomorphic and
Therefore can be compressed
into tiny cardboard boxes
Though some are kept,
in gilded ones.

We fill the shallow
edges and rigid-mitred corners
Threatening to spill out
But never daring to,

For one cavalier drop
brazen enough to leap the confines
Pulls the mass
gelatinous, oozing
As though it were whole
to the floor

Soiling the feet of
the Box/er
To then be discarded.

The Conformer

(recited with tap in synchrony)

If . . .
If I . . .
If I walk . . .
If I walk the pattern that you set . . .
  you tell me . . .
If I walk the pattern that you set . . .
  living in a box . . .
You tell me . . .
that I am . . .
You tell me . . .
  I can be . . .
But one day
  When you weren't looking,
When your words fell from my
    ears
      I forgot —
        and flew.

The Projector

First to you. Long prior to my first
glimpse of light, to my first gasp of breath
I knew you had no desire for me. You seem surprised.
Do you really think that you whose blood coursed
thru my veins could hide that you never wanted me?
      The days of ''no'' the days of ''not now''
the days of ''not there.'' It is because of you that
every time I reach, I'm rejected. You keep me
helpless.

And you — no not brutal, not overt, just
cold, passive, indifferent. Life whips you
like the wind on the willow. And you sway
blindly. How could you invite me to be when
you never were? You taught me passivity well —
it is you who keeps me helpless.

And to you — Creator of the quagmire of meaninglessness.
Where is the abundance — the healing? How has the
myth of Providence manifested to me?
      It is I who keeps you . . . no . . . I mean . . . you
      It is you who keeps me . . . I . . .
      It is I who keeps me helpless.

" i fell into a numbness
til the only tree I could see
took me up in her branches
held me in the breeze
made me dawn dew . . .
i found God in myself
and I loved her
i loved her fiercely. **"**

       Ntozake Shange

From Ntozake Shange's *For Colored Girls Who Have Considered Suicide When The Rainbow is Enuf:* Bantam Books, New
York, 1977.

The Meaning of Suffering

Anna Polcino

- • When Do We Suffer? • Pain
- • Assumptions in Medicine • Health Embraces Illness
- • The Disabled • Mental Illness • Why Me?
- • Biblical View of Illness • Surrender — Affirmation
- • The Meaning of Suffering

Sister Anna Polcino, S.C.M.M., M.D., founder and international psychiatric director of the House of Affirmation, International Therapeutic Center for Clergy and Religious, is a member of the Medical Mission Sisters. Dr. Polcino received her degree from the Medical College of Pennsylvania. Following a surgical residency at Hahnemann Hospital, Philadelphia, she worked for nine years as a missionary surgeon and medical director at Holy Family Hospital in Pakistan and Bangladesh. Dr. Polcino then returned to the United States, completed a psychiatric residency at Worcester State Hospital, and pursued further postgraduate medical studies at Harvard University. A member of the American Psychiatric Association, the American Medical Association, the Massachusetts Medical Society, and the National Federation of Catholic Physicians, she is current editor of the Bulletin *of the National Guild of Catholic Psychiatrists. Dr. Polcino is consultant and lecturer to clergy and religious in the United States and abroad.*

Introduction

It is not easy to write about suffering. When we have truly suffered or ministered to suffering persons, the experience and the mystery of suffering leaves us stunned and awed. It is beyond the words of reason. As a surgeon in the culture of Pakistan and Bangladesh and a psychiatrist in my own culture, I deal with suffering as an inevitable part of being human. Suffering is part of the human condition. When I reflect on suffering, I look at life — its anguish and agony, its ecstasy and joy. Even in ecstasy there is suffering. Think of St. Teresa of Avila. She suffered so in her moments of ecstasy that she even asked God to spare her further mystical experiences. Suffering is all encompassing. It includes oppression, poverty, war, imprisonment, acute and chronic physical, mental and spiritual illness, loneliness, heartaches, soul-aches and death. It comes to all of us, rich and poor.

When Do We Suffer?

There are some experiences, some situations when we do not suffer even though we experience pain. (Think about the winner of a 100-yard dash.) In other pain-free situations, we suffer when we see circumstances we can not immediately change. (Think about the flashes of economic disadvantage and racial hatred that dot our consciences.) In our culture, we look for immediate relief of suffering. (Consider the number of advertisements for aspirin and other pain-reducing remedies.)

Suffering in general is a state or a process of severe distress associated with events that threaten the integrity or wholeness of a person.[1] Therefore by definition, suffering is human. Animals experience pain, but not suffering. Animals are not capable of self-reflection or self-transcendence. To understand suffering, we have to understand what it means to be a person.

Personhood has many parts. Personhood is more than body, mind and spirit. Each individual is born with certain genetic factors that may include a predisposition to illness. Each of us has personality traits and character; a cultural background; roles and a relationship to ourselves which includes a self-image, a body-image and a self-concept. We also have certain relationships to others and to God. In addition, we have a secret life, an unconscious life.[2] All these aspects are parts of a person. Therefore, any physical, mental or spiritual illness is not only a specific trauma to one aspect or another of a person but also a trauma to the person as a whole.

This is evidenced by the fact that some people have a high threshold for pain while others can be overwhelmed by a simple headache. I have a high threshold for pain, both physical and mental. Part of the reason for this is my Italian cultural background and my childhood experience of being reared by my aunt who suffered many adversities. She had great faith and devotion to many saints. Whenever difficulties presented themselves, she would always say, "Dio vide e provede." God sees and provides. She meant that in God's good time the situation would be taken care of. Sometimes we could do something about it and other times we were to wait and bear the situation.

In the disease of leprosy, the ill person has no pain because the bacillus of leprosy injures the nerve fibers. For a long time, doctors thought that the disease caused fingers to decay. But the truth was that rats could eat away at the hands during sleep causing fingers to fall off or be eaten away. No pain was felt. Also, if leprous persons lifted something or turned a door knob, they could exert more force than needed because pain was not there to limit the amount of force to that which would not do injury. But, lepers' greatest suffering is not from the disease but from their isolation from society and their loneliness of heart. This emotional pain in turn does damage to their self-esteem. We can treat the disease of leprosy, but often we fail to treat the dis-ease of the leprous person.

I remember when I was in Bangladesh I went up to the northern part to Dinagpur for a rest. But once there I did not rest because the Sisters of Charity from Milan, Italy, took me to see a leper colony. When I got there we sat and talked to the lepers, had tea and visited with the bedridden members. The doctor for the colony came only once a year. The superior said to me, ''Doctor, the doctor is not coming for many, many months. The fingers of one of the lepers are practically falling off him. Would you do something?'' I amputated. That was my first experience treating a leper, a surgery that required no morphine because my patient felt no pain.

But what would usually be considered dramatic surgery did not emerge as the important aspect of the day. What was most memorable and important was our visiting — our sitting and drinking tea and encouraging the lepers. I shook the hands of those who could shake hands. I was not afraid of them. I treated them as people. Our visit brought solace not only to the lepers but also to the sisters who minister to them.

Pain

To be without the capacity for physical pain is not a good thing for humans. Perhaps the painlessness of leprosy makes it in a way a particularly inhuman affliction. Pain, whether it be of the body or of the mind, alerts the sufferer that all is not well. It says, pay attention. In pain, both the body and the mind tell us something about ourselves. Pain is a warning sign. For this reason, sometimes having a high threshold for pain may not be a good thing. Pain keeps us from the point of pain that is detrimental.

In 1981, I continued to travel for workshops in spite of lower back pain caused by pressure on the nerve roots because of osteoarthritis. I did not pay attention to the message of my body. Finally I had to listen as I became more incapacitated.

Sometimes we think the greater the pain, the greater the suffering. This is not always so. For example, ask a woman after childbirth if the pain caused her suffering. Most of the time, she will not even remember the pain because of the beautiful reward of an infant. But ask a woman who has not been able to bear a child: she will speak of her suffering and so will the husband. Theirs will be a mental suffering because of what they perceive as their incapacity with its attendant guilt, in addition to whatever other meanings they attach to the situation. Even celibates who willingly choose not to marry can experience a kind of mental suffering at never having their own child. As humans, we would like to see something of ourselves live on. Such reflection and perhaps mental pain often occurs in mid-life for the celibate, the childless, and even parents because mid-life marks the end of certain possibilities for all of us.

The mental pain of mid-life is fairly certain and common but we can suffer when we do not know the cause of pain. Not knowing the cause of pain can be troublesome as we then imagine all kinds of serious illnesses, particularly if one is a physician or nurse. In 1964, I had serious pain in my left arm. At the time, I was helping the cook in preparing meals for a hundred sisters. I had to lift heavy cauldrons of soup and tea. For several days, I was diagnosing myself, ''Perhaps I tore the brachial plexus?'' Finally, I saw a neurosurgeon who said I had a ruptured disc and a spur due to osteoarthritis and that I would need surgery. Just before surgery, he reminded me that with a slip of the knife, he might paralyze me at surgery! This was an added suffering, even though I then knew the cause of the pain. So knowing the cause of pain can cause suffering also. For this reason, doctors and nurses can make poor patients.

Consider the patient with cancer. Bodily pain can be a problem but the mental suffering or anguish is far worse. The patients are confronted with their own death. They suffer a loss of energy; the many changes or losses in relationships; the fear of abandonment; and a host of other things. The mental suffering of persons who are told they have cancer is far greater than the physical condition itself. When the physical pain gets to be too great, something can be done. Pain medication can offer relief which in turn can help the mental suffering of cancer patients because they know there is relief to be obtained. But we need to convey support as well so that they will not feel abandoned.

> People in pain frequently report suffering from pain when they feel out of control, when the pain is overwhelming, when the source of pain is unknown, when the meaning of pain is dire (terminal cancer) or when the pain is chronic.[3]

Assumptions in Medicine

Some of the assumptions on which medicine is based today are that the cure of disease is more important than the care of people, and that death is the worst thing that can happen to a person. These assumptions are questionable. Consider the terms "health," "disease" and "illness." What do they mean? The present medical model defines *disease* as any departure from health. To be sick means to suffer from disease. *Health* is defined in the dictionary as "physical and mental well-being, freedom from defect, pain, or disease." We in traditional medicine still view people as dualities, bodies and minds. Although there is a trend now in medicine to view individuals as bodies, minds, and spirits within a social context. This approach is called the holistic health approach or point of view.

Eric Cassell has described illness as "a state of being, feeling and unfitness." He suggests that we should use the words "illness" to stand for what patients feel when they go to see a doctor and "disease" for what they *have* on the way home from a doctor's office. In the African culture, health and illness have to do with relationships. The Shona people greet each other in this way: "How are you?" and the person replies, "I am well if you are well." There is a Zulu proverb that says: "When there is a thorn in the foot, the whole body must stoop to pluck it out.'' Here we can see the biblical concept of the mystical body. If you suffer, I suffer. The whole person participates in the illness of an injured part.

Participation in illness differs in cultures. In our western culture, we look for causal relationships, the objective or scientific facts. In African cultures, subjective or spiritual meaning and inherent relationships are considered important. We take sick persons away from their families and put them into hospitals with another world of experiences and apparatuses that cause more suffering. Traditional African medicine cares for the sick wihin their tribe. They treat through interpersonal relationships. Again our view is objective, the African, subjective. One is not necessarily better than the other. There is a need for both, a holistic concept of health. Perhaps the best prescription for health is sharing what we are, and what we have, with others.

This approach to health is of paramount importance in suffering. Karl Stern in his autobiography *The Pillar of Fire* spoke of the study of pathology as the science of suffering. When we look at a microscope slide of liver tissue in which there is cirrhosis, we do not stop at the slide and its pathological information but think of the person from whose liver it came. One frequent cause of cirrhosis is alcoholism. Reflect on the suffering alcoholism causes for alcoholic persons, their families, co-workers and friends. In a religious community or rectory, alcoholism causes suffering also.

Health Embraces Illness

Excluding illness from the concept of health is, in itself, not healthful. Health bespeaks wholeness and integrity and must include and embrace illness as part of its harmonious integration of the many aspects of the business of living. Sickness reminds us that living includes: suffering and pain; confronting and dealing with the ugly; going through the frustrations and struggles that are part of the process of growth and change until we die. Living or health is *to be on the way* and not to have arrived.

For some reason people regard good health as a right. They resent the headache or cold that makes it impossible for them to keep up with work or play. They resent the pain and inconvenience that remind them that they are not completely self-reliant, and that destroy the notion that here on earth everything should go as human beings plan. Consider a person who faces a long and debilitating illness. Both the patient and the family bring to this situation all their past associations with illness and their emotional attitudes. They can feel discomfort, anxiety, fear, depression, anger and despair. Relationships may change; family or community patterns will shift; all kinds of defenses will be set up; and the new situation may trigger unexpected emotional responses.

Resentment often accompanies illness. Patients usually resent the loss of competence and independence, and the feeling that they are not in control of their lives. If you reflect on your times of illness, you will find that the hardest thing was that you were not in control and that a certain dependency was necessary. The family may feel resentment also at its loss of privacy and the invasion by the professionals involved in the patient's care. Friends may avoid visiting because they do not know what to say or feel helpless to give support to the patient.

I experienced this when I was in bed for several months in pelvic traction. People would come to visit and were at a loss for what to say. One person said, "Whatever do you do all day?" My answer was, "I am not *doing* but *being* for a change." Some people feel helpless and cannot wait to leave. Some, like Job's friends, give all kinds of advice. Sometimes the patient feels more like an "interesting case" than a human being. Those around the patient may feel vulnerable emotionally and may erect a facade of coldness or indifference.

Patients, their family and community may experience fear of the unknown. This is a cause of suffering. Sometimes there is anger at human frailty. Sometimes because of illness, a wall rises between a husband and wife, or there is a distancing with parents and children, or with community members or those in authority. Misunderstandings occur.

The Disabled

Different disabilities involve different problems and challenges for the disabled person. A number of recent books and movies depict disabled people who have overcome their handicaps. These success stories suggest that in order to be affirmed disabled people must compete, *and win,* not only with themselves and among their peers but also with healthy people. Such success stories feature exceptional disabled people. Ordinary disabled people often live lives of frustration, ongoing struggle, and diminished self-respect. Programs of rehabilitation, which aim to develop capacities enabling disabled people to have a certain measure of independence and perhaps even be able to support themselves economically, are only a first step toward what most of us consider an ordinary lifestyle. Society's prejudice is a constant challenge to the disabled to accept themselves and to live and act in a world that can be non-affirming and cruel. The disabled can know great suffering.[4]

Edward R. Walsh makes the following point:

When we label the disabled and put them into categories, then truly we are handicapping them by not allowing them to use their talents freely. That's why I try to look upon the disabled as "handi-capables." By focusing on abilities, we confer dignity through our attitude; we communicate confidence in their courage to overcome the condition that limits them.[5]

People who consider themselves healthy look on disabled people as different. Sometimes disabled persons spend much of their lives trying to conceal what makes them different from so-called normal people. They often meet new acquaintances in an atmosphere of emotional stress where they are greeted in a confused and awkward fashion, sometimes with disgust and rejection or pitying protectiveness. When confronted with a very obviously disabled person, many people do not know where to look and in an effort to avoid their own pain, they look in every direction but at the disabled person. This kind of reaction minimizes the disabled person's qualities, and lessens everyone in such encounters. Those who minister must look at the entire person and not focus on, and then away from, the handicapped aspects. In this way, we see disabled persons in an integrated way and will not add to their suffering.

John J. Gavin in *Concerning the Employment of the Disabled* states:

> What the disabled have going for them is this: the manifestations of disability are sometimes difficult for the casual observer to accept, because the casual observer looks upon these phenomena as tragedies. But those who must live within the physical limits of the disability develop a capacity to struggle and adapt. And that capacity provides the means to make life whole and coherent, even if painful and inconvenient. That is what we really have going for us: we have a reason for being, we have a reason to do a first-class job. So we can perform well under circumstances that other people may find trying.[6]

Every handicapped person must go through an identity crisis. They must adjust to a new body at the same time they are suffering the loss of their former body image. They wonder who they are and who they will be.

Space and distances to the healthy person are not constant daily difficulties, but to the disabled person they may become overwhelming trials. I had the opportunity to experience this both in myself and in one of my patients. When I had surgery on my lower back in 1982, I found getting out of bed to go to the commode an insurmountable distance and even worse the idea of the distance from the bed to the lavatory only ten feet away in the hospital room. After having experienced this myself, I could truly understand one of my patients who had an amputation of her lower leg due to diabetes. For her to get out of bed with her prosthesis and use the commode was quite a trial. I remember saying to her during one of my hospital visits, "Sister, it's a terrible distance," and she looked at me and said, "Yes, how do you know?" I could truly empathize since I had had similar experience. My sharing of what distance had meant to me, gave her courage. It took many months before she could conquer such distances.

In fact, any great suffering, no matter the cause, brings about an identity crisis in the individual, for the suffering touches not only the self-image but also the self-esteem and self-concept of the person. The sufferer must undergo a process that involves the gamut of the suffering emotions — denial, anger, anxiety and depression. The process may take only a few months or it may take years. Finally, in people who grow and change there is a new wholeness, a new identity, and in others there is a stagnation, a resignation. They may be unable to find any meaning in life.[7]

Mental Illness

Although suffering from any physical condition affects the mind and spirit, mental illness causes greater suffering both to the suffering person and to those others in relationship to the sufferer. An acute psychosis can be a devastating experience for the individual. So much is at stake — their social, economic and spiritual life. A psychiatrist will work vigorously to bring the person to reality by use of anti-psychotic medications. Psychotic suffering is destructive and not to be endured. Everything possible must be done to obtain better mental health.

Emotional suffering can lead to despair. Such despair causes suffering in the observer too. Often deeply depressed people see suicide as their only choice. It is terrible suffering to be locked in one's self and isolated. This kind of suffering calls for active participation of the observer or those surrounding the individual. This suffering is not meaningless. It can lead to a fuller knowledge of self-acceptance and to a peace in the light of faith.

Why Me?

Anyone who has suffered will have asked the question, why me? Why have I been chosen to bear this suffering, this illness? Not all will formulate the question so clearly. Some will deny it. Some may be so disturbed in confronting this question that they experience more confusion and disorientation. Suffering touches the very root of existence. People will tell you, when they see the pain or suffering you are in, that "God loves you very much. He chastises those He loves." When I hear this I say to myself, "I wish he would not love me so much." However, pain makes us re-evaluate our lives with a reorientation toward deeper values.

If we face the question, why me? it can lead to a deep learning experience. I remember, when studying psychiatry, we were told that in psychotherapy, never to ask patients why they did something. In general, *why* questions in human affairs are unanswerable. The better questions to ask are: what can I become, what can I do, and how will I do it now that I am in this suffering state? Suffering people do not really expect answers. But through thought and action they may find their personal meaning for why they suffer. We ought not view suffering as a problem to be solved, but a state to be experienced. It is a mystery. It is a human experience that we can do something about sometimes, and other times all we can do is just be in the suffering.

Biblical View of Illness

In the Old Testament, illness was looked on as God's punishment for sin and his vengeance on evil-doers. If the chosen people were faithful to the law, they could expect health and prosperity. If they were unfaithful, they were punished with illness and misfortune. For the Israelite, the fundamental sin was an attempt to build a personal greatness without regard for God. Thus, in the Psalms, one who was sick and knew he had sinned would lament but not complain. Illness was a harsh reminder of human limitations, of the universal law that in life we suffer and die.

The Book of Job further examined the suffering of the innocent. Fidelity to God demanded more than observing God's laws; it meant trusting God's love and affirming whatever he sent. Suffering and illness were seen as introducing a special relationship with God and promised God's call to a deeper and purer realization of that relationship.

Christian interpretations evolved that saw illness and suffering as tests, conditions meant to lead a person closer to God. Illness and suffering became the sign of grace and the symbol of the Messiah (Isa. 52-53). In the New Testament, although Jesus healed the bodily ills of many, healing was not his primary concern. His healing was meant as a sign, but suffering and sickness remained, linked with Christ's death, resurrection, and transfiguration. For the Christian, illness and suffering mean sharing in the very reality of Christ's redemptive suffering. Christian suffering contributes to the transformation of the world. It shares in the world's longing for Christ's triumphant Second Coming. Sickness itself has already been healed by Christ. Sickness is meaningful.[8]

We can make suffering meaningful if we look at what we give to life, our creativity. We can become creative through suffering. We should consider what we take from life through awareness of our experiences and experiential values. Too our attitudinal values, the stance we take in most difficult situations, give meaning to our suffering.[9]

No matter how terrible the situation we may be in, we are
still free to take a stance, either positive or negative. And if we
cannot find immediate meaning, it does not follow that there is
no meaning. We will have to focus beyond ourselves to find
meaning in particular situations.

When I came home from Pakistan in 1968, because of arthri-
tis and chronic liver disease, I could not understand the meaning
of my illness. It was a few years later that it became clear. It
was in God's providence that I do another, different ministry
— study psychiatry and establish the House of Affirmation for
my brothers and sisters in religious life. To help them to become
psychologically and spiritually healthier persons and to help
them find their meanings in their suffering. To understand the
meaning of suffering is to surrender to a suffering. It may
require an act of faith and trust for a time, because we cannot
understand everything immediately. It may mean you have just
to bear the suffering amidst your questions. But at the same
time, look at your faith — is the Holy Spirit trying to tell you
something?

Surrender — Affirmation

Acceptance of, or surrender to, or affirmation of particular
suffering involves active participation by the sufferer. It is not
resignation, or a passive stance, but an integration of the situ-
taion into the life plans of the person. However, acceptance is
never achieved in one leap. It is an ongoing process that grows
toward affirmation. Persons growing toward affirmation begin
to have some peace; there is active cooperation in the healing
of their suffering. This is so important in recovery that physicians and those around the sufferer must be careful of any negative remarks. After my surgery, I went to see the
neurosurgeon. I still had pain, almost as bad as before surgery.
The surgeon was dismayed as I went in for my examination to
see me walking with a cane. He then told me that perhaps he
had not removed enough bone and that I might need further

surgery. This threw me into a depression for the next month. It delayed my recovery.

The Meaning of Suffering

I cannot prescribe meaning to my suffering patients but I can describe what is going on so that they may be aware of other values or alternatives available to them through understanding. Closing one's eyes to suffering, will not remove the suffering. We may be surprised to find that limitations in one area can open us up to an expansiveness in some other area. For example, a paraplegic may develop the intellectual and spiritual aspects of her life. If death were the end of all, then suffering seems meaningless nonsense. But our Christian faith tells us otherwise.[10]

We can give a general meaning to suffering in that God in Christ is our ultimate goal, our ultimate meaning. We do not look for the suffering to be removed but we look to Christ who suffered as our source of strength. Since suffering is always a personal matter, each of us must find the possibilities in the reality of our particular suffering to find our own personal meaning. Meaning in suffering has to do with responsibility to one's self and to God. We make a commitment with God's grace. Nothing great or important can be accomplished without some sacrifice which entails suffering. It has been said that one can ascertain the success of a project by the amount of suffering it entails. Or that one can be reassured that God's blessings and his will are there in a particular ministry or task by the sufferings endured along the path. Saint Teresa Avila tells us, "His Majesty rewards great services with trials, and there can be no better reward, for out of trials springs love for God."

Suffering helps us to grow in patience and generosity. We learn how to live through suffering in patience which is a waiting — a waiting upon the Lord. Suffering can lead to contemplation. It teaches us to trust in the Lord. Present suffering builds on our past suffering so that reflection on how we got through any previous suffering reminds us that God is always present. This strengthens our faith. We then see that suffering is redemptive. ''If God is with us, who can be against us?'' We develop a certainty of faith. Cardinal Medeiros, who suffered much, said, ''Whatever God wants.''

We learn to be thoughtful and sensitive toward ourselves and others. Although each suffering is a personal, unique experience, we can better empathize with others who have a similar suffering. Suffering calls forth our creative imagination either in ourselves or from others. It calls forth our compassion which is a sense of shared suffering.

The meaning of suffering is that we are not isolated beings. We need companionship; we need human support and compassion. We need others to talk with about our feelings, our fears and anxieties, and our hopes and our dreams. We need to be listeners to one another. We need to share one another's strength. At least Job's friends did listen to him, even though afterward they gave him all kinds of reasons and advice for his sufferings that caused him more suffering.

We learn that life is precious; that we ought not to waste it but make it count. We cannot become truly holy without suffering. No matter what our sufferings are, physical, mental or spiritual, they are the raw material for holiness. Our sufferings are the experience of the desert, but even the desert is not totally barren. There are living creatures and desert flowers. Father David Doiron, our staff psychologist at Hopedale, said, when we were discussing suffering, ''Yes, we could not have an oasis unless there was a desert.'' So too, our suffering can lead us to find the flowers and the oasis.

Someone has said that every essential form of spiritual life is marked by ambiguity. This observation is certainly true of the Christian who finds life in death, joy in suffering, and strength in weakness. It is also the way God chooses to come to us. Bonhoffer observed that God is weak and powerless in the world. He took our sicknesses and carried our diseases for us. Thus it is not by his omnipotence that Christ helps us but by his weakness and suffering. Christ chose the way of weakness as the way to be with us, because it is the human condition. In the suffering of Christ, we recognize a true man, and in that recognition, we realize that it is foolish to dream of ever being completely free from suffering, from our own weakness. I believe this acceptance is good, for our weaknesses, our fears, even our sins can be the very stuff out of which holiness is made. What is the raw material of the dark night of the soul but our sins and our failures?

So we have to learn to use our weaknesses as Christ did by accepting them freely as God's will for us. Our affirmation must be after the manner of Christ. Christ did not redeem us by dying, but by accepting his suffering and death. Did you ever think about that? Because he was human, Christ was going to die anyway. He redeemed us because he accepted the death of crucifixion. It was a human act of freedom. He accepted all the sufferings. I feel Christ's greatest suffering was not the crucifixion but the suffering he endured and affirmed in the garden of Gethsemane. In that hour, he affirmed all that would come later.

Now if we Christians are to become Christlike, then the same act of loving free choice must be at the very center of our whole consciousness. We want to choose to love everything that we do and everything that we are though we are weak. Accept human frailty as God's way of making saints of us. Accept it as a way of identifying with Christ the victim. Accept it as God's way of reminding us of our dependence on, and need of, him. Affirming our sufferings, we can offer them to God as the only things we can truly call our own. We can offer them to God as an area where he can show his mercy. I often reflect that I am grateful God is going to judge me because I can depend on God's mercy. He will be just, yet he will always temper his justice with mercy.

So we offer these sufferings and weaknesses as our share in the weakness and the passion of Christ. Paul could glory in his weaknesses, and in spite of them he could trust in God. "He who trusts in the Lord finds nothing but mercy all around him."

The result of this affirmation and this offering is an undisturbed peace, no longer a neurotic search for means to sanctity. Rather, we use the raw materials at hand to become holy, to see them and ourselves as God sees them and us, to offer all to him and to be patient with the whole world, but most of all with ourselves. You may remember the last entry in the diary of George Bernanos' country priest.

> It's all over now. The strange mistrust I had of myself, of my own being, has flown, I believe, forever. That conflict is done. I am reconciled to myself, to the poor, poor shell of me. How easy it is to hate oneself. True grace is in forgetting, yet if pride could die in us, the supreme grace would be to love oneself in all simplicity as one would love any member of the body of Christ. Does it really matter? Grace is everywhere.[11]

Saint Therese, the Little Flower, observed that everything is a grace. I suggest her as a model. Saint Therese had a compulsive personality. The most difficult thing for a compulsive personality is to give up control or to surrender. One of her greatest sufferings was to surrender. If you really believe in that spiritual philosophy of life, no matter what happens, both joys and sorrows will have meaning for you. You will find God speaking to you. I suggest this prayer to Saint Therese that the House of Affirmation says for nine days in preparation for her feast.

O Eternal Father, Whose Infinite Love watches
    in Wisdom over each day of my life,
Grant me the light to see in sorrow as in joy,
in trial as in peace,
in uncertainty as in confidence,
the way Your Divine Providence has marked for me.

Give me that faith and trust in Your care for me,
so pleasing to You in Saint Therese of the Child Jesus,
and I will walk in darkness as in light,
Holding Your hand and finding in all the blessings
I receive from Your loving bounty,
that "Everything is a grace."

Amen

Endnotes

1. Eric J. Cassel, M.D., "The Nature of Suffering and the Goals of Medicine," *The New England Journal of Medicine,* Vol. 306, No. 11 (March 18, 1982): 639 – 645.

2. Ibid., pp. 641 – 643.

3. Ibid., p. 641.

4. *See* Leonard Bowman, *The Importance of Being Sick* (Wilmington, N.C.: Consortium Books), 1976, Chap. 10.

5. Edward R. Walsh, *Ligourian,* May 1981, p. 47 quoted in Richard Wozniak, C.M.F. and Placido Rodriguez, C.M.F., "Some Thoughts on the Admission of Handicapped into Religious Life" (Chicago, NCRVDM), nd.

6. John J. Gavin, *Concerning the Employment of the Disabled,* p. 127, quoted in Richard Wozniak, C.M.F. and Placido Rodriguez, C.M.F., "Some Thoughts on the Admission of Handicapped into Religious Life" (Chicago, NCRVDM), nd.

7. Jurrit Bergsma and David C. Thomasma, *Health Care: Its Psychosocial Dimensions* (Pittsburgh, Penn.: Duquesne University Press, 1982). *See* especially chapter 1, "The Body and the Self," pp. 1 – 18.

8. *See* Bowman, *The Importance of Being Sick,* pp. 21 – 39.

9. Viktor E. Frankl, *The Will to Meaning* (New York: New American Library, 1969), pp. 50 – 79.

10. *See* Flavian Dougherty, C.P., ed., *The Meaning of Suffering* (New York: Human Science Press, 1982).

11. George Bernanos, *Diary of a Country Priest* (New York: Carroll and Graf, 1984), p. 299.

WARNING: Suffering May Be Hazardous To Your Health

J. William Huber

• Aspects of Suffering • Suffering Isolates Us or Unites Us
• Perfect-People Pain and the Religious Life
• Causes of Self-Inflicted Suffering • What To Do

*Reverend J. William Huber, Ph.D., is assistant director and
full-time psychotherapist at the House of Affirmation in Web-
ster Groves, Missouri. A priest of the diocese of Pueblo, Col-
orado, Father Huber received his undergraduate education at
St. Thomas Seminary in Denver. He completed graduate work
in marriage counseling at the University of Detroit, and
received his doctorate in clinical psychology from the California School of Professional Psychology in San Diego. Before
joining the staff of the House of Affirmation, he was the found-
ing director of the Pueblo Diocesan Office for Family Life.
Father Huber also served in various other pastoral and associate pastor positions before undertaking his graduate studies.
He is a member of the American Psychological Association,
the American Association of Marriage and Family Therapists,
and other professional organizations.*

It is Autumn 1983. The trees outside display brilliant shades of yellow and red. Radio and television reports recount tragic events. More than 200 U.S. and 50 French military men have died during a "peace-keeping" mission in Lebanon. Grenada has been invaded. Suffering has engulfed many people directly and news of them involves both their individual families and the whole world family.

In my daily encounter with the therapeutic community, I am touched by the lives of the Church's wounded healers. As I reflect upon my work, I sense these wounded healers resemble the autumnal changes of nature outside. These hurting brothers and sisters are uncertain of where the winds of change will take them during the winter of their therapeutic journey.

Some of these men and women describe their lives in terms of "being dead." Others come with only a faint glimmer of hope — clinging to the idea that the therapeutic community will be their only chance to overcome the forces that entrap them. Many look forward to the day they will be completely healed, no longer having to suffer, and able to return to their ministry. Some hope to find a magic pill or potion that will dissolve the suffering in their daily living. Others may expect the therapies themselves to resolve hurts. Each in different ways seeks to overcome suffering.

Those nearing completion of their therapeutic journey still may sense suffering, but their perspective on it has changed from the day they fearfully walked through the front door. Now they may be apprehensive that the delicate growth begun may be snuffed out or lost as they resume their ministerial works.

The communities to which many wounded return look forward with expectation to a completely healed person. Some mistakenly expect a perfect healer to return. A few others may appreciate the toll that the trauma of suffering inflicts.

All of them in their own way, and I in mine, wonder why God permits suffering, especially the suffering of "peace-keepers," of innocent islanders, and of wounded church leaders. The Old Testament author of the Book of Job struggled with the same issue at the time of the Israelites' exile. Writing about his lived experience, the author of Job reflected — as we do twenty centuries after Christ — upon the question of why just people suffer while evil people seem to prosper. Would it not seem more realistic and appropriate if those who seek perfection prospered? Today many of us seek meaning to personal suffering and grief whether our own or that of humankind.

Aspects of Suffering

Suffering comes from many situations and sources. Suffering may involve the anguish of loneliness, unhappiness, dreams destroyed, hopes frustrated, feelings of being discounted, or of innocence lost. The casualties include not only those wounded physically by war or spiritually by the loss of a loved one, but also those who have lost direction in life or who, caught off balance amid technological change, lose the work-path they have devoted their lives to following. Many religious and lay persons alike still suffer the wounds of confusion following the Second Vatican Council. Vatican II casualties may be found in every diocese, community and parish. And they suffer.

Women, particularly professed women religious, suffer today as they struggle to be accepted as equals in a church structure that seems threatened by their mere presence. Church men suffer from male insecurities, questioning the motives of their female equals. Contemporary humans continue to experience the anxieties of previous ages, just when many thought Vatican II would bring the Church closer to perfection in our own day.

Many attempts have been made throughout history to understand the origin of suffering. At least three origins have been identified as the cause of suffering. The first view attributes human suffering to God. Another points to human beings as the source of human suffering. A third way attributes suffering to the devil, or the world. Each attempt to explain human suffering falls short and provides only a partial answer.

If you can recall ever saying to yourself — if not aloud — "How could God do this to me?" you may be attributing suffering to God. One may also voice this belief by stating: "Nothing happens without His willing it." To ascribe the causation of suffering to God is to make God the source of evil. How does one reconcile this idea with a God who creates out of love, not out of malice?

The view which attributes suffering to God may lead one to give up belief in an all-powerful God. Ben Kushner, author of the book *When Bad Things Happen to Good People*, notes that the author of the Book of Job believed in God's goodness as well as in Job's goodness. The resolution of this conflict of suffering thus is resolved by the author of Job who "is prepared to give up his belief . . . that God is all-powerful."[1]

This views God as quite imperfect — a personal God who cannot prevent unfair things from occurring in one's life. Thus one encounters a philosophical problem beyond the scope of this reflection on suffering.

The friends of Job arrive at a different reason for Job's suffering. "God grants prosperity to the righteous and punishes the wicked with adversity; therefore Job is a sinner"[2] is their view of suffering. These wise men applied the collective teaching of wisdom to the individual case, erroneously "ascribing all evil and suffering to human malice." Some biblical scholars object because the application of a collective teaching to an individual case is inappropriate.[3]

Who among us is so old as to forget being warned during one's youth that "God sees what you are doing." One may have developed the idea of God as an accountant who keeps perfect records for each person, and whose interest is in balancing each person's debits and credits through meting out punishment for evil. Thus, one is the cause of one's own suffering.

Is this not masochistic? Would one really inflict suffering upon oneself? Does one draw the same conclusion as Job's friends who ascribe "all evil and suffering to human malice?"[4]

It may be more comfortable to understand suffering as punishment for sins, because this enables one to see the world as predictable and orderly. Most people desire to live in a predictable and orderly world.

It is on the basis of needing a predictable world that some people go so far as to excuse a rapist on the grounds that "the woman was provocatively dressed and deserved her fate." And it is out of a need for a predictable world that some persons today believe that people on social welfare programs, food stamp programs, or aid to dependent children programs are the cause of their own suffering. "If they were not so lazy, they would not be so poor," is the response of people desiring an orderly and predictable world. Moreover, by blaming the victim, one can feel reassured that people cause their own suffering and one's own world is not a bad place after all.[5]

Job was not comforted by being blamed. Those suffering on welfare are not comforted by this view either. Job knew he was not evil. Thus Job arrived at a different conclusion: "The justice of God" is not "realized in the existing world."[6]

Many people mention being trained in the "school of hard knocks." These people see suffering as educational. Others attribute suffering to free will. As long as humans are free to inflict harm upon others, there will be suffering.

Finally, in the search to find a satisfying reason for suffering, "bad luck" is seen by some as the source of suffering. Unfortunately, "too many Christians still believe that suffering has a value in itself."[7] Bothered by the "dis-ease" of suffering, it is only human to seek meaning in this common experience.

Suffering is the "common companion of birth and growth, disease and death, and is a phenomenon deeply intertwined with the very question of human existence."[8] Perhaps the only thing more difficult than to suffer is to see one's loved ones suffer and be unable to reduce their pain.

Thus, Job-like contemporary humans attempt to arrive at an understanding of suffering, pain and dis-ease. The solution Job arrives at is not an intellectual one, but experiential. One arrives at the meaning of suffering only by living with it and reflecting upon it.

Suffering Isolates or Unites Us

Human imperfection is at the root of all suffering. Perhaps that is why so many seek perfection. Like the impatient prayer of one Christian, "Lord, make me a martyr, but make it quick!" Who wants to suffer?

Suffering may cause one to feel isolated. There is no suffering like that of feeling one is all alone. "Underlying all suffering is the fact that human beings are needy. They do not have the sources for their strength and life within themselves."[9] They feel isolated. Suffering forces us to turn toward community. Yet at the moment of suffering, one may find it most difficult to reach out and seek one's community. Because of this people tend to become all the more alienated from others, and suffer in addition from illogical comparisons to others or an unrealistic need to see themselves as perfect.

Comparison is a disservice both to oneself and to others. For a large scale example, there are men and women in our country upset with the government's reaching out to peoples in foreign countries. They ask why the U.S. needs to be a "peace-keeper." Others wonder why our country tries to help feed people at home who seem unconcerned about overpopulation. Many in our land question whether our country has "suffered" enough at the hands of imperfect nations and careless people. False comparisons create dis-ease with our neighbors far and near.

The universal experience of suffering afflicts the rich and poor alike; wealthy nations as well as Third World countries; the communist block nations as well as nations devoted to democratic ideals. Making comparisons between peoples avoids discovering meaning in common human experience.

To seek meaning in one's suffering is to enter a reflective process — a process of growth and maturation. And to explore meaning in one's suffering is an invitation to be gentle with oneself and to reject doing violence to oneself.

Perfect-People Pain and the Religious Life

Let me explore more in depth only one of the many ways in which clergy and professional religious may invite needless suffering into their lives. The invitation comes under the guise of being called to perfection.

The call to religious or clerical life is as varied as the people who respond to that call. For many, that vague, inner sense that God was directing them toward a life of perfection seemed difficult, but not impossible. The challenge to be perfect may have seemed to be the only real choice at that time.

Whatever the invitation that drew them toward religious vocation, they expected the ultimate gain to be the salvation of their soul. Intermediate goals seemed to be included in that call as well, goals such as friendship and the support from others with similar goals. But the implied hope was that by following the way of perfection, they would receive eternal rewards. And to reach that reward, the customary training involved performing one's duties ever more perfectly day after day. That was the ideal set forth by traditional spiritual writers such as Thomas à Kempis in his *Imitation of Christ*. "Consider the Hidden Judgments of God Lest You Become Proud of Your Own Good Deeds,"[10] is the title of his fourteenth chapter of Book III, sounding a warning about pride and evoking a call to be perfect lest God punish one's imperfections.

Unfortunately, much of the traditional pursuit of perfection seemed more productive of suffering than of health, happiness or maturity. A certain masochistic behavior was equated often with perfection. "Unquestioning submission to pain and suffering is masochism. We can learn nothing from suffering unless we question it and work through it somehow."[11] But questioning one's suffering was seldom if ever encouraged; nay rather it was highly discouraged, and many times became a cause for dismissal from religious training.

Practices such as "Particular Examens" too often focused upon negative situations, upon what wrong one did rather than upon positive actions and interactions. How many persons increased their suffering as a result of such a focus may never be known. Psychologists have found that negative rewards foster certain behaviors rather than correct them. Thus paying attention to one's faults can be quite rewarding of "faulty" behaviors, and tends to maintain them, rather than help get rid of them.

Older members of religious communities will remember how "penances" were meted out to help develop perfection. Sometimes well-meaning superiors required the performance of meaningless tasks in the pursuit of perfection. Little wonder that film director Fellini had such success with some of his themes on religious community living. The plots were not fiction but were being lived out by some religious communities.

One can argue that religious practices were not so distorted as I may be picturing them, or that these practices did encourage a more open and self-giving attitude by which individuals could identify more with the sufferings of Christ. Nevertheless, I invite the reader to reflect upon the helpfulness of pursuing perfection solely through the price of suffering. "Suffering does not necessarily lead to love. . . ."[12] The pursuit of *perfectionism* may have been the goal rather than the pursuit of *perfection* in the lives of many in years gone by. But perfectionism may not be a value worthy of pursuit.

Clinical research suggests that "perfectionism may be one of the key psychological factors predisposing certain people to painful mood swings."[13] I doubt whether professional religious suffer more painful mood swings than the general population, but I suspect that for many religious, the roots of their dis-ease lies in perfectionism. These persons suffer as a result of their perceived failure to be a "good" religious. They see only their inadequacies in living their lives. Many expect themselves to be more perfect than those they serve. Little wonder they become depressed when they admit they experience human shortcomings. These disappointed perfectionists suffer a loss of self-esteem and a sense of personal stagnation. When such feelings of failure or inadequacy are triggered, they may experience a loss of self-worth "that can trigger episodes of severe depression and anxiety."[14]

Interestingly, "perfection is man's ultimate illusion. It simply does not exist in the universe. . . . It's only an abstraction, a concept that doesn't fit reality."[15] While the concept of perfection may be useful in this world, it would appear to have inflicted much needless suffering upon well-intentioned people by well-meaning individuals who confuse idealism with reality. Such an equation has led to undue stress and suffering. Would it not seem fitting to caution users of such spirituality: "Warning: Suffering May Be Hazardous To Your Health" — your physical, emotional, and spiritual health.

Cigarettes today, known as carcinogenic agents, are required to carry such a warning on their packaging. Yet the cancer of needless suffering resulting from unrealistic expectations, may well be as dangerous an affliction to personal health and well-being.

In pursuing perfection, one fears being judged imperfect. Only God knows how many thousands of religious men and women were trained through such fears of being sent home from their seminaries or novitiates. Was the suffering realistic, or was it necessary? Most people tend to see themselves as imperfect and unacceptable to others. When poor self-concepts are confirmed by those in authority, little wonder individuals suffer non-redemptive pain.

The error in this thinking is the belief that perfection joins one person to others. Just the opposite is true: human imperfections connect people to one another. Acknowledging imperfections "has the spiritual power to break down barriers between people in order to make them reach out to each other in mutual support and communion. In suffering, we experience new kinds of fellowship, often beyond our expectations. . . ."[16]

Individuals' imperfections and human qualities make them similar to other humans. Yet how many of us go through life believing that if others knew what we are really like, they would surely reject us.

Social psychological research indicates that competent, superior people are generally liked more when they occasionally blunder and appear human than when they never stumble. Others need to feel similar to an individual in order to connect. Little wonder that perfectionism can be deadly in interpersonal relationships, although religious might tend to expect just the opposite because their training has reinforced the idea of perfectionism.

We all need to discover and try out new ways of thinking about reality and the goals we had planned to accomplish. Seldom, if ever, does the reality of our lives produce difficulties. Rather it is the way we think about or interpret reality that is our problem.

Causes of Self-Inflicted Suffering

What seems to create a lot of self-inflicted, needless and unproductive suffering is an all-or-none way of thinking about life. For example, if all-or-none persons are not appointed to a hoped-for position, they choose to believe they are total failures. It is either/or for these men and women. They have yet to discover that people exist only in the reality between these two extremes. It is a very lonely existence at either of the extremes.

Self-inflicted suffering is experienced too by those who overgeneralize their way of looking at the world. These people prefer clear-cut realities. Be aware of the use of "everyone" and "no one" in conversation. For example the priest who thinks he will "*never* become a pastor" upon discovering another priest has been chosen over him causes suffering of his own making. He has over-included all life events in one negative incident. Such over-inclusion — generalization — creates self-hurt and masochistic pain.

Unrealistic expectations, rather than realistic hopes, create needless dis-ease. Truthfully, is there really such a thing here and now as an "ideal" or "perfect" world? For some religious, unrealistic expectations create needless suffering. The blanket expectation that all religious sisters *should* wear a religious habit continues to create unnecessary suffering. Whose expectation is it anyway — yours? or somebody else's? Behind such an expectation may be the idealized hope that the return to the religious garb will signify a Church once again effective and believed in by modern people.

Many clergy and religious have an idealized expectation that they will arrive at a day when they no longer will experience the anxiety of sexual feelings or temptations. Such an unrealistic ideal produces only needless, personal suffering and failures. Would it not be more productive and far less pain-filled for such people to focus upon what one can learn from the struggle with these temptations instead? "Libidinal impulses are, to be sure, perverted by this stance, but they are not destroyed."[17]

We would like to believe that such self-inflicted suffering and pain would encourage perfectionists to extinguish their habits and give up trying ever harder and harder. In reality, the opposite seems to occur. Because of habitual rigid reinforcement, they continue to strive and suffer.

We can compare that process to the gamblers' experience. As they hover over one-armed bandits in gambling casinos, gamblers live in the eternal hope that the next pull of the lever will bring the jingling sound of the jackpot payoff rolling into their laps. Hope springs eternal. The idealist always hopes to leave behind human defects. Such a person lives in the eternal expectation that "next time" things will be "perfect." It is the way of those who sincerely believe they will never again be tempted to evil.

Obviously, there is nothing inherently sick or pathological or even sinful about setting high goals for oneself, provided such goals are realistic and can bring ease with life. But such goals need to be determined selectively and not anticipated for each and every instance.

Cognitive-behavior therapists tell us that reality does not cause troubles or suffering when realistically faced. True, reality may produce anxieties. But *how one interprets* reality is what causes suffering. Likewise it is simply not enough to understand the problem. I continue to be amazed at how individuals attend workshop after workshop in the eternal hope that the more knowledge they amass, the more they will overcome their sufferings. Knowledge and understanding do not resolve personal dis-ease. Only a change in *thinking* about reality will do that.

In my experience, many clergy and religious tend to live in a fantasy world. How many therapy hours have I listened to suffering people talk about how easy it is — not it "seems easy" but "it is easy" — for others to speak out in group settings and community meetings, and "how easy it is for others" to be self-confident. But the person in the therapy chair before me believes he or she will *never* be able to arrive at that stage of growth.

It is a fantasy that others experience little or no difficulty in their lives. The more we dwell upon our own insufficiencies, the more inferior we will feel. The more unrewarded we feel, the more dissatisfied we become. Suffering can be a self-perpetuated way of thinking.

Self-inflicted suffering definitely is hazardous to one's health. But such suffering need not be irreversible, nor unto death. Self-inflicted suffering is a mental construct, a way of bringing useless suffering upon one's self.

What To Do

One of the ways out of such suffering is to look at what is gained from maintaining such thinking. What are the rewards? Does such a pattern help one avoid change? Perhaps known suffering is better than unknown. It outweighs the fear of change involved in rethinking one's behavior and pattern of living.

Another way to free ourselves from self-imposed suffering is to test out our assumptions about life. What will happen if we lower our aims from idealistic to more realistic and achievable goals? Frequently the result is more effective and satisfying living.

For example, does a "perfect" sermon really bring about more happiness than preaching a "well-delivered" but incomplete sermon? Incidentally, have you ever heard a "perfect" sermon, or read a "perfect" novel? Does performing "exceptionally" guarantee happiness or an end to suffering?

Does anyone really know the "perfect" response to make to a mother whose son has just been killed, or to a man whose wife has just died?

Lurking behind our suffering for perfectionism is generally fear. We may fear that our suffering will never end. We may fear disapproval or failure. Such fear is a gnawing, miserable feeling worse than a sharp pain.

If you have ever suffered from the gnawing fear that you have forgotten to lock a car or a house, to turn off a gas stove or a TV, you have known gnawing fear in a mild form. But such fears can also loom large.

Some men and women suffer immensely because of needless self-inflicted doubts and fears. Despite precautions of all kinds, these people never rest. All avenues of possible oversight have to be explored to protect them and others from possible harm. Who appointed such a worrier to be custodian of the world? The only way out of this type of suffering seems to be *to refuse* to give into the self-inflicted habit of fear. Such persons must learn to live with anxiety until fear loses its grip.

These individuals need to allow their feelings to catch up with the most realistic thinking of which they are capable. What Religious Sister during the 1960s did not sense some anxiety on that day when the community's traditional habit was modified or became optional?

I recall a Sister-friend who told me about dressing in a contemporary dress on such a day. For the first time in years in modern dress, she sat on the edge of her bed and cried. She worried about coming downstairs in her own convent and appearing in front of her own community! She started to remove the dress and to return to the more familiar habit — but then stopped herself and gently, but firmly, *made* herself return to the contemporary dress and walk downstairs with great fear and trembling. Her behavior and thinking had changed, but it took many more days and other situations for her to be more at ease with her new behavior.

Self-imposed suffering flows from maladaptive thinking. The risk involved, the negative assumptions, the unrealistic expectations all tend to keep us trapped in the role of being the suffering servant. *Events* do not inflict pain, but our *interpretation of events* can create states of dis-ease.

Every human being makes mistakes. The basis for this generalization is the reality of creation. We are all less than perfect. We all make mistakes. But mistakes need not be sources of suffering. Rather, they can be opportunities for growth and maturation. You and I learned to walk, and to talk, and to eat, and to read by making mistakes. We learned because of mistakes. Consider the idea: Happy Are They Who Can Make Mistakes And Learn From Them.

The self-imposed suffering I have attempted to examine need not exist. To the extent that personal emotional upset is caused by distorted thoughts, then to that extent each of us is responsible for our own suffering.[18] In such self-imposed suffering, a more responsible way to suffer would be to place boundaries upon suffering. We need to be willing to stop suffering. We need to shorten our self-imposed sentences to expire immediately.[19]

Obviously not all suffering is self-inflicted. Some pain does have external causes as we constantly witness in our everyday world. This suffering may not be understood. It can only be lived out on a day-to-day basis of acceptance and challenge; by daily attempting to find meaning in its reality. ''We may not be responsible for the suffering into which life has thrust us, but we are entirely accountable for the attitude we choose.''[20] Any other approach than conscious choice of attitude toward suffering seems to be masochistic.

It is not difficult to criticize Christian masochism, since it has so many features that merit criticism: the low value it places on human strength; its veneration of one who is neither good nor logical but only extremely powerful; its viewing of suffering exclusively from the perspective of endurance; and its consequent lack of sensitivity for the suffering of others.[21]

We all need to grow up and mature through our suffering. But we need not look for it where it is not. "How we cope with suffering depends on our maturity, and both suffering and maturity are important subjects for religious experience. . . ."[22]

WARNING: Suffering can be hazardous to your health, *especially if it is self-inflicted*. Who needs it?

Endnotes

1. Harold S. Kushner, *When Bad Things Happen to Good People* (New York: Avon Books, 1981), p. 42.
2. John L. McKenzie, S.J., *Dictionary of the Bible* (New York: Macmillan, 1979), p. 441.
3. Ibid.
4. Ibid.
5. Kushner, p. 39.
6. McKenzie, p. 441.
7. Louis Evely, *Suffering* (New York: Herder and Herder, 1967), p. 76.
8. David Bakan, *Disease, Pain, & Sacrifice* (Chicago: University of Chicago Press, 1968), p. 57.
9. Arthur C. McGill, *Suffering: A Test of Theological Method* (Philadelphia: Westminster Press, 1982), p. 34.
10. Thomas à Kempis, *The Imitation of Christ* (Milwaukee: Bruce Publishing, 1940), p. 112.
11. Charles C. L. Kao, *Psychological and Religious Development* (Washington, D.C.: University Press of America, 1981), p. 320.
12. Evely, p. 77.
13. David D. Burns, ''The Perfectionist's Script for Self-Defeat,'' *Psychology Today*, November 1980, p. 34.
14. Ibid.
15. David D. Burns, *Feeling Good* (New York: New American Library, 1981), p. 309.
16. Kao, p. 318.
17. Dorothee Soelle, *Suffering* (Philadelphia: Fortress Press, 1975), p. 22.
18. Burns, *Feeling Good*, p. 180.
19. Burns, *Feeling Good*, p. 184.
20. Kao, p. 318.
21. Soelle, p. 22.
22. Kao, pp. 314 and 315.

Suffer Thy Neighbor:
The Marching Song

Audrey E. Campbell-Wray

- The Global Marching Song
- The National Marching Song
- Our Neighbors' Marching Song

Audrey E. Campbell-Wray, Ph.D., director of education for the House of Affirmation, has graduate degrees in theology from St. John's University, New York, and in applied spirituality from the University of San Francisco. She received her master's and doctoral degrees in clinical psychology from the Psychological Studies Institute in Palo Alto, California. Dr. Campbell-Wray is a psychotherapist, art therapist, and spiritual director, and has conducted numerous workshops and retreats on issues of psychological and spiritual health and growth. She is a member of several professional organizations including the American Psychological Association and the American Art Therapy Association.

Given the 1980s rising tide of oppression, I have chosen to share these psychotheological reflections from the point of view of the oppressed who can wait no longer.

> We shall overcome, we shall overcome
> We shall overcome, someday.
> Oh deep in my heart,
> I do believe
> We shall overcome, someday.
>
> Truth shall make us free
> Truth shall make us free
> Truth shall make us free, someday.
> Oh deep in my heart
> I *want* to believe
> We shall overcome someday. [1]

What is the essence of my nostalgia for that wonderful chant? It reminds me of a faith no longer innocent and the aura of a time of hope for America compromised by recurrent experience with oppression in the midst of other forms of human inhumanity, and their export, worship, and adoration.

Last summer as I watched two of my nieces play with their collection of Barbie dolls, I observed a reality so painful that both my eyes and my heart cried for many days. They were involved in the distribution of these dolls and it was very clear that one particular doll was not wanted, had no status, no desirability. Here were two beautiful, young black girls, not yet twelve years old, and the rejected doll was the only black doll in their collection. They had learned well the lessons of institutionalized racism.

Belonging to the fellowship of the weaker means that we are inclined to suffer. We are vulnerable in a way that means permitting ourselves to be touched where it hurts, accepting forgiveness for sin. It is due to the author of such merciful love that we are called to affirm and nurture the life, dignity and self-esteem of every person. People are so very precious and

so very easily destroyed. We are the only species who sense-
lessly and systematically destroy one another; and we are the
only species "full of grace."

   In these reflections on the senseless and systematic destruc-
tiveness of injustice and oppression, some issues of injustice
will be mentioned as will some victims of oppression. I will
speak primarily of the black experience, because that is my
experience. But oppression is a universal experience and you
may wish to consider the experience of Hispanics, Asians,
South and Central Americans, the poor, the rich, the mentally
ill, the homosexual, women.

The Global Marching Song

We must keep in mind the global, national and personal impli-
cations of power structures that foster oppression. If we get
close enough to the truth of these structures, will that truth
make us free?

   Let us try on some truths for freedom's sake. Freedom, of
course, is not free. The shackles of oppression are wound
tightly and locked by systems of economic gain. For example,
American and British financial power is invested in the Repub-
lic of South Africa, an insidiously oppressive country. Would
the government collapse in a matter of days if Western invest-
ment were withdrawn?

   There are 4.5 million white South Africans and 27 million
black South Africans. The white South Africans own 87 percent of the land. Black South Africans must have passes even
to walk on that land and cannot congregate on it. They have
been herded onto "homelands," a euphemism for useless, arid
land. By being declared citizens of these various "homelands,"
black South Africans are effectively removed from the political
structure of the republic-at-large and disenfranchised.

   The United States supplies South Africa with 40 percent of
its oil and oil by-products, 70 percent of its business machines,
and 27 percent of its transportation. In South Africa we find

Colgate Palmolive, General Motors, American Motors, IBM, Burroughs. Are they underwriters of the tyranny of South Africa?

Consider one of these American corporations. General Motors has a contingency agreement with the South African government stipulating that if the black South Africans rise up against the tyranny that fills their daily lives, the General Motors guards will join with the South African government troops to put down the insurrection. Furthermore, corporation plants can be converted to munitions production if an insurrection occurs. It can happen. It did happen in Germany under Hitler. Our government has sent shock-batons to be used by South African troops to maintain ''orderliness.''[2]

If we get close enough to a truth, will that truth make us free?

Let us try on a little more truth for freedom's sake.

Grenada is about one-fifth the size of a Congressional district. It is a tiny island of relatively poor post-colonial black people. I personally know three people whose parents were killed by American bombs. That makes six of the ''only eighteen'' people our government said we killed when we bombed this tiny island. The British Broadcasting Corporation reported we killed at least one hundred people when American bombs destroyed a mental hospital and its nearby environs.

The National Marching Song

Consider the disturbing question, Who is my neighbor? as we briefly seek another kind of more personal truth for freedom's sake.

On August 27, 1983 more than 300,000 people stood, once again, by the reflecting pond in Washington, D.C. We had stood there twenty years before dreaming with Martin Luther King, Jr. Isn't this the same dream wandering?[3] Who were our neighbors singing the same marching song?

What truth will make us free?

In June 1983, *Ebony* magazine ran an article by Jerry Thompson, a veteran reporter from Nashville, Tennessee, who for sixteen months infiltrated and lived as the title of his book suggests *Inside the Ku Klux Klan*.[4] The knights of the Ku Klux Klan, according to Thompson, are alive and well in the United States of America, enjoying the sympathies and financial support of middle- and upper-class Americans who are not public about their membership support. The Klan has become a family affair featuring klansmen, klansladies, and the Klan Youth Corps. The Klan boasts that it is well armed and has groups in the United States military, throughout the nation, and throughout the world.

Will truth make us free?

Enforcement of affirmative-action is rapidly vanishing in the 1980s.[5] The U.S. Labor Department is discontinuing its policy of reviewing company compliance with the equal employment opportunity laws before awarding contracts.

Dr. Beverly P. Cole, NAACP National Education Director, lends some truth, as reflected in the title of her piece, to another national situation, *The State of Education for Black Americans*.

> In most inner-city schools, where approximately 75 percent of black students are in attendance, achievement levels are usually two or more years behind the national norm.

Studies have shown that black children tend to drop below grade level in elementary school and fall further behind as they get older, until, at age sixteen, at least 35 percent are below their modal grade.

Many theories have been offered to explain this disgrace; most built upon the notion of "blaming the victim." "Cultural deprivation," "the culture of poverty," "the deficit model," "the disadvantaged" — all explain why the low socioeconomic student could not overcome the problems of poverty and social pathology and be expected to learn.

Nevertheless, the results of the "effective schools" research clearly demonstrate that children can be educated successfully, regardless of their family background. However, one of the main prerequisites is a belief and expectation on the part of the teacher and principal that this feat can be accomplished. Schools must demonstrate respect for the dignity of all students and be committed to the principle that all students are educable, regardless of their race or economic background.[6]

Indeed! Will the truth make us free?

Our Neighbors' Marching Song

Once we choose to look at the suffering of our neighbors caused by injustice and oppression, our inner moral drive toward integrity compels us to look deeply within ourselves. Passive cooperation with injustice and oppression comes from within and is in some psychodynamic fashion a derivative of our own self-hate. There is a New Testament wisdom repeatedly reminding us that our lives and our world will remain disordered as long as we foster or ignore disorders within.

When is the last time you filled your own hands with your own compassion? touched your own self gently? or held your own inner wounds?

The task is to seek wholeness and unity within; unity with creation; unity with global humanity; unity with the Creator. Essential elements of this task are: to seek unity with our weaknesses so that acceptance, warmth and love might strengthen us; to seek unity with our hidden self so that love might transform; to seek unity with our neighbors so that our life and our neighbors' lives become one as our suffering and our neighbors' suffering becomes one. So enmeshed are we with one another that if I am not free, humanity is not free. If my neighbor is not free, I am not free.

The suffering caused by injustice and oppression is precisely the same on a minor scale as on a major scale. We can start with the people with whom we live and examine the subtleties of bigotry in our own home, our own family, including religious community and rectory living. When we look at church structures, what do we see in terms of female human beings? When we look at church and community structures, what do we see in terms of human beings of racial minorities? When we look at our neighborhood, our town or our city, can we recognize institutionalized racism in the fabric of these societies? Are the places where we live and work integrated and just? What is our responsibility in the face of what we see?

It is my responsibility to know my neighbor. It is my responsibility to love my neighbor. It is my responsibility to see to justice for my neighbor. It is my responsibility to be willing to live next door to my neighbor. If God is not in my neighbor then God is nowhere! If my neighbor is suffering and I do nothing, then I am shouting, "Crucify Him, crucify Him." Rather, I should sing my neighbor's marching song because until my neighbor can live with dignity, freedom and justice, there is no dignity, freedom or justice for me . . . or for you.

> We are marching abreast, four by four.
> We are marching to death, strange war.
> There's a bone and a body, more and more.
> There's a child who is hungry, what for?[7]

Endnotes

1. Lyrics adapted from traditional Civil Rights marching song.
2. Lecture notes, Randall Robinson, Executive Director, TransAfrica Forum, Washington, D.C.
3. *I Have A Dream Speech,* Martin Luther King, Jr., March on Washington, August 1963.
4. Jerry Thompson, "Inside the Ku Klux Klan," *Ebony,* Vol. XXXVIII, No. 8 (June 1983): 100.
5. *The Atlanta Constitution* (Atlanta, Georgia), 6 April 1983.
6. NAACP, untitled editorial, *The Crisis,* vol. 90, no.5 (May 1983): 42.
7. Lyrics: "We are Marching Abreast" by Audrey E. Campbell-Wray. Used with permission of Audrey Elizabeth Arts. © 1969.